1978

PEOPLES OF THE EARTH

volume nine

Southern Africa

Including Madagascar

THE DANBURY PRESS

(Preceding page) Southern
Africa is a region of vivid
contrasts. Bustling cities
and the trappings and cares
of urban life are unknown by
this Muila girl of Angola.

The publishers gratefully acknowledge help from
the following organizations:
Royal Anthropological Institute, London
Musée de l'Homme, Paris
International African Institute, London
British Museum, London
Royal Geographical Society, London
Scott Polar Research Institute, Cambridge
Royal Asiatic Society, London
Royal Central Asian Society, London
Pitt-Rivers Museum, Oxford
Horniman Museum, London
Institute of Latin American Studies, London

Editorial Director **Tom Stacey**

Picture Director **Alexander Low**
Executive Editor **Katherine Ivens**
Art Director **Tom Deas**
Assistant Editor **Elisabeth Meakin**
Project Co-ordinator **Anne Harrison**
Research **Cheryl Moyer**

Specialist Picture Researcher **Diana Eggitt**
Picture Research **Claire Baines**
Elly Beintema
Jeanne Griffiths
Emma Stacey
Editorial Assistants **Richard Carlisle**
Rosamund Ellis
Minette Marrin
Susan Rutherford
Xan Smiley
Pamela Tubby
Design Assistants **Susan Forster**
Richard Kelly
Cartography **Ron Haywood**
Illustrations **Sandra Archibald Ron McTrusty**

Production **Roger Multon**
Production Editor **Vanessa Charles**

PHOTOGRAPHIC CREDITS
Cover – **Lucien Offenberg, Rene Burri** (Magnum from the John Hillelson
Agency), **John Bulmer, Tony Carr** (Colorific), **Alexander Low, Black
Star, London.** 2, 3 – **Lucien Offenberg.** 14, 15 – **Rene Burri** (Magnum
from the John Hillelson Agency). 16 – **Mansell Collection.** 17 – **Peter
Carmichael** (C.S.M. Pictures). 18 – **The John Hillelson Collection.**
19 – **Jan Kopec** (Camera Press). 22 – **The John Hillelson Agency, Peter
Carmichael** (C.S.M. Pictures), **Paolo Koch** (Rapho, New York), **Paul
Popper.** 23 – **Peter Carmichael** (C.S.M. Pictures). 24, 25 – **Hamilton
Wright** (F.P.G.). 26, 27 – **John Bulmer.** 28 – **Paul Popper.** 29 – **John
Bulmer.** 30, 31 – **Ian Berry** (Magnum from the John Hillelson Agency).
32 – **Rene Burri** (Magnum from the John Hillelson Agency). 33 – **Tony
Carr** (Colorific). 34, 35 – **Brian Seed** (The John Hillelson Agency).
36 through 38 – **Ian Berry** (Magnum from the John Hillelson Agency),
exc. bot. rt. 36 – **Rene Burri** (Magnum from the John Hillelson Agency),
and bot. rt. 38 – **Philip Jones Griffiths.** 40 – **Peter Carmichael** (C.S.M.
Pictures). 41 – **John Bulmer.** 42 – **John Moss** (Colorific), **Bob Youngleson.**
43 – **John Bulmer, John Moss** (Colorific). 44 – **Ian Berry** (Magnum from
the John Hillelson Agency). 45 – **Alice Mertens.** 46 – **Terry Spencer**
(Colorific). 49 – **Terry Spencer** (Colorific), Daily Telegraph. 50 – **Gerry
Cranham** (Rapho, New York. 51 – **Basil Humphries, De Beers
Consolidated Mines Ltd.** 52, 53 – **Peter Carmichael** (C.S.M. Pictures).
54 – **Brian Seed** (The John Hillelson Agency). 55 – **Winn Swann**
(Camera Press). 56, 57 – **Peter Carmichael** (C.S.M. Pictures) exc. bot. lt.
56 – **Paul Popper.** 58 – **Alice Mertens, John Moss.** 59 – **Peter Carmichael**
(C.S.M. Pictures). 60, 61 – **Paul Popper.** 62, 63 – **John Bulmer.** 64 – **Ian
Berry** (Magnum from the John Hillelson Agency), **Peter Carmichael**
(C.S.M. Pictures). 65 – **Brian Seed** (The John Hillelson Agency). 69
through 71 – **Maurice Bloch.** 72 through 85 – **Alexander Low.** 86, 87 –
Hoa Qui. 88 – **Alexander Low.** 89 – **Maurice Bloch, Alexander Low.**
90, 91 – **Alexander Low.** 92, 93 – **Maurice Bloch,** exc. bot. rt. 93 –
Alexander Low. 92, 93 – **Maurice Bloch,** exc. bot. rt. 93 – **Hoa Qui.**
94 through 103 – **Philip Jones Griffiths.** 104 through 107 – **Lucien
Offenberg.** 108, 109 – Aspect Picture Library. 110, 111 – **Alice Mertens,**
exc. bot. rt. 111 – **Lucien Offenberg.** 112 – **Alice Mertens.** 114, 115 –
Black Star, London. 116 – **H. Pager.** 117, 118 – **C. S. Larrabee**
(Transworld Features). 119 – **Hubertus Kanns, Nat Forbman** (Life
Magazine), **C. S. Larrabee** (Transworld Features). 120, 121 – **Alice
Mertens, Jungen Schadeberg, F. Balsan.** 122 through 125 – **Alice
Mertens.** 120, 127 – **Cloete Breytenbach.** 128, 129 – **Alice Mertens.**

The DANBURY PRESS
a division of GROLIER ENTERPRISES INC.

Publisher
ROBERT B. CLARKE

Printed in Italy by
Arnoldo Mondadori Editore, Verona

901.9
P421
g

Contents

Supervisory Editor of the Series:
Professor Sir Edward Evans-Pritchard,
Fellow of All Souls, Professor of Social Anthropology,
University of Oxford, 1946-1970,
Chevalier de la Légion d'Honneur

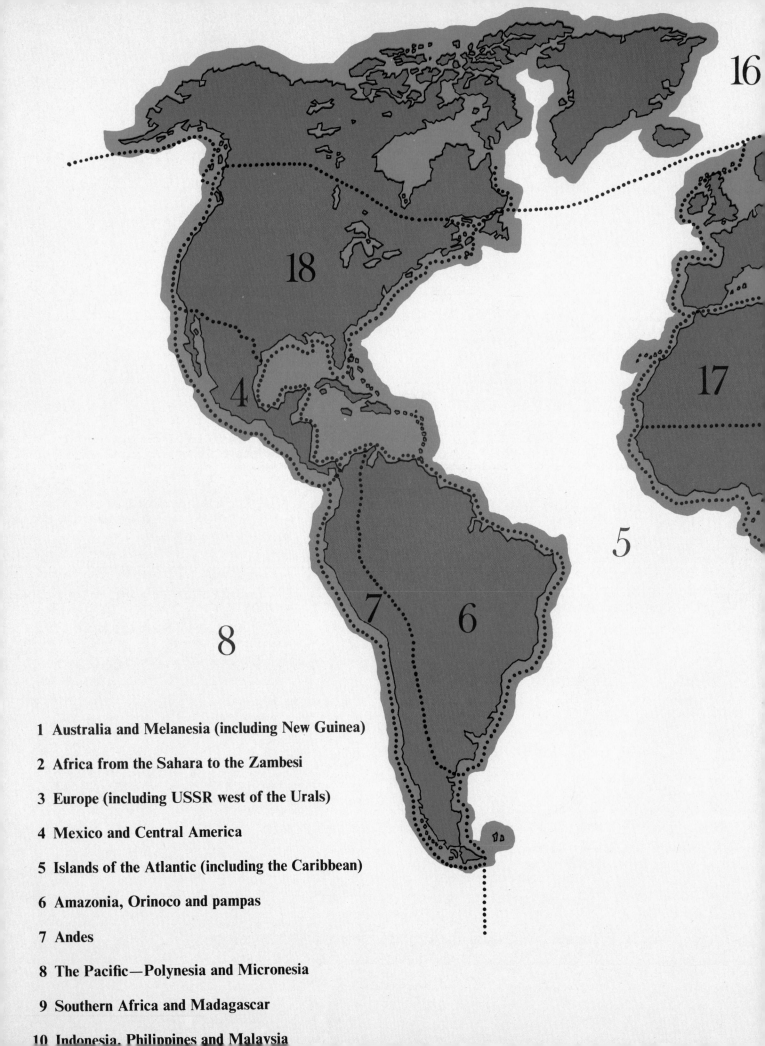

18

17

4

5

7   6

8

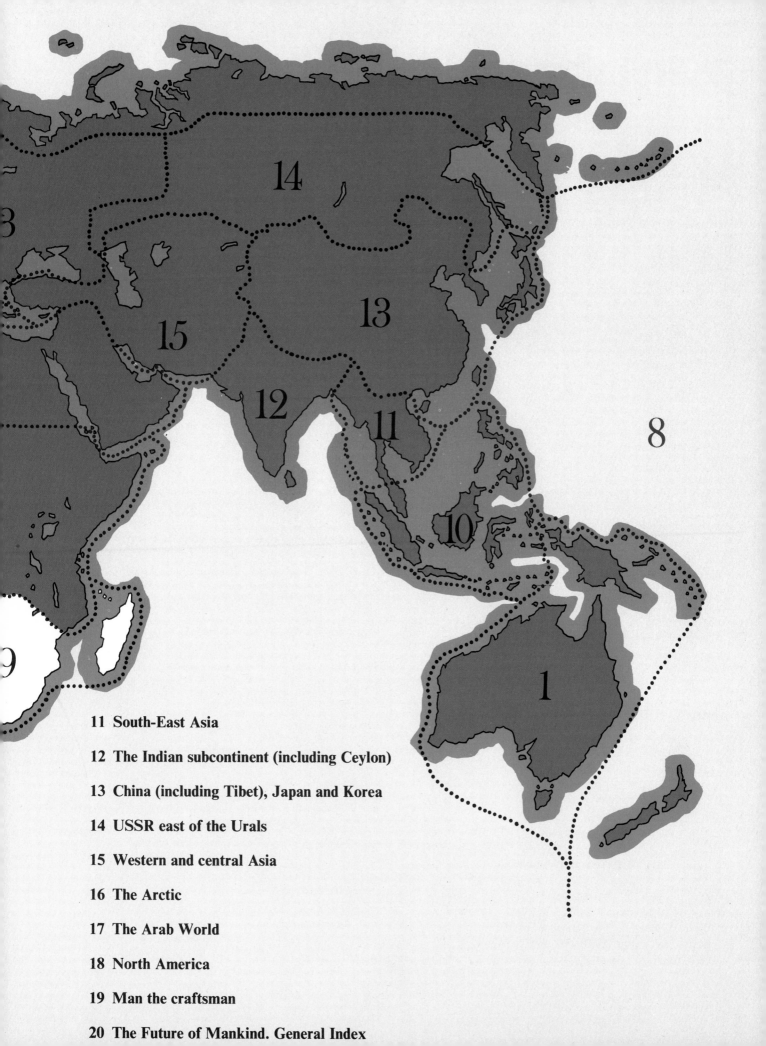

Marriage and Affinity

Many of the marriages contracted by the peoples of Africa today are at least nominally Christian or Muslim. This results from Mohammedan invasions and infiltrations on the north, east and west coasts, and later from the arrival of Christian missionaries in the African continent. The marriages in Africa which are neither Muslim nor Christian are designed to legalize the status of children, but do not aim to control or legalize sexual relationships. Normally in Africa every child has some sort of legal status, and at least until recently there was no such thing as an illegitimate child. The fact that a mother has never been married does not prevent a child having a legal status from the moment of birth. Consequently Africans everywhere are unable to understand how members of the so-called civilized races can talk about illegitimate children.

About twenty per cent of African tribal groups have up to eight different legal forms of marriage, most of which derive from earlier widespread legal forms which have been replaced. Most Africans practise a form of legal marriage in which the couple are financially bound to their parents. This form of marriage is common among Bantu-speaking, Nilotic or Hamitic groups, and involves what is often mis-named the payment of 'bride-price'. By this anthropological writers usually mean the payment of animals or other wealth by the bridegroom's relatives to the bride's relatives. In fact this form of marriage does not involve a payment of bride-price, for although the bridegroom's relatives do make payments to the bride's family, this is not the purchase of the bride in the English sense of the word, nor was it ever a final transaction. Some anthropologists have written about payment of 'bride-price' by instalments, believing that the payments were in effect purchase by instalments of the wife (or wives) if the parents of the bridegroom were not rich enough to pay immediately.

This is a wholly false concept of the transaction in normal African marriages. The payments are never final, no matter how wealthy the parents of the bridegroom might be. The real significance is not purchase, but a guarantee of the stability of the marriage – particularly of the legal status of the wife's offspring. Normally the marriage insurance, a more appropriate term than 'bride-price', continues to be paid until all the children are adult. Once the marriage has been contracted and the woman has given birth to a child, it is extremely difficult to dissolve the marriage legally, or obtain a divorce. The husband's family is bound to continue payments of marriage insurance and to have a full share of responsibility for the growing children.

Dissolution of marriages and divorce are both frowned upon and rare, because of the effect on the legal status of the children. However, it is perfectly normal to find couples whose sexual relationship has broken down completely, but who are still jointly responsible for the well-being, education, housing, clothing and health of the wife's children even though these children might have a different physical father. The payment of marriage insurance is in no way linked with the sexual relationships of the couple who have been legally married.

The transactions involved in marriage insurance are negotiated by the couple's respective parents or, if necessary, by their legal guardian. The point of marriage insurance is to guard the interests of the children. Although marriage also implies normal sexual relations between the partners, this was an entirely private matter and outside the contract. In fact, though this attitude has become less common recently, the two people involved in a marriage ceremony prefer that at least one of the children born to them should have a different physical father.

Soon after a marriage a woman may refuse ever to have a sexual relationship with her husband and, though married to him, thereafter have children by other men until she ceases to be of child-bearing age. Nevertheless all these children, regardless of their actual parentage, rank legally as the husband's children. It is his responsibility and his family's to support them, feed them, clothe them and make marriage arrangements for them.

In some tribes, once a girl is married legally she proceeds to have children on her husband's behalf even though it could well happen that for five or six years she never sees him, or sleeps with him at all. This, for example, is true of the Masai of East Africa: as long as the man is still a member of the warrior class, it is illegal for him to have sexual relations.

Marriages are further stabilized by family pressure. Once a girl is married and has children, if her parents feel that she is acting in a way which might break up the marriage, the family unit, they will do everything in their power to persuade her not to act irresponsibly. They will remind her that she could have other sexual partners if she liked without breaking up the family. It is in their interest to protect her marriage for if it is shown that she has destroyed the marriage they will be required by law to hand back to the bridegroom's family the increments on the payments. These will be computed as one animal for each year of marriage.

Marriage insurance also means that the husband will act responsibly towards his wife's children. If a final breakdown of a marriage can be shown in court to be the husband's fault then his family will not be able to

Louis Leakey

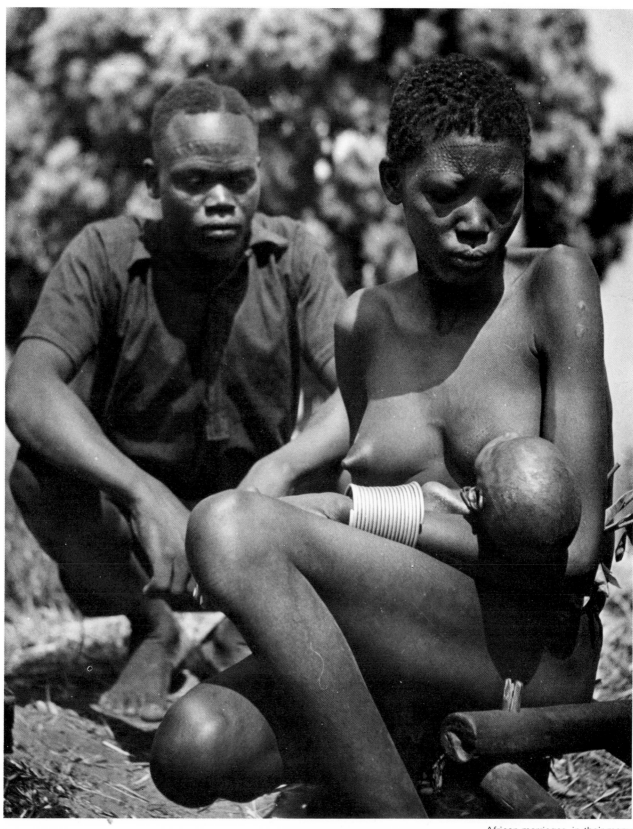

African marriages, in their many
different forms, do not control
sexual relations, but provide
security and status for all
the children of a community.

recover any of the marriage insurance. So the husband's parents are also careful to see that their son does not break up the marriage.

Of the other legal forms of marriage in African societies, the most important is the ancient custom among Bantu-speaking peoples by which the legal marriage of a number of young women is arranged with an older, married woman who takes on the legal status of a man. Until recently in many African tribes a higher proportion of girls than boys normally survived to marriageable age. This situation has traditionally been met by the practice of polygamy. Some young women of 23 or over who have failed to find husbands content themselves with becoming second or, more rarely, third or fourth wives. They then enjoy almost the same status as the first wife except in religious ceremonies in which the first wife participates with the husband. Polygamy, as it does not meet the needs of flighty and unstable women, cannot however provide for all the excess women, such as unstable girls who might be expected to break up their marriages. There has always been, instead, another widespread satisfactory custom. A limited number of married women go before the tribal authorities and go through a ceremony whereby legally they become men. Physically they remain women, continuing to have normal sex relations and leading normal family lives with their children. Meanwhile they marry a number of butterfly girls. The community often helps them by providing the necessary marriage insurance for the families of these girls, and helping to provide homes, clothing and food for the wives. When the marriage is complete the girls can start having children by any man of their choice, although the 'female father' is the legal father.

There are also two common forms of legal marriages which meet the needs of the young man who lacks living parents or near relatives and so has little chance of raising the necessary continuous insurance payments for normal marriage. He goes before the elders with the girl who is willing to marry him, accompanied by her parents, and opts for a matrilocal and matrilineal marriage. The couple then live together as a normal married couple, but their home is attached to the bride's and not the bridegroom's household and the children take the name of the wife's clan and sub-clan. Alternatively he goes to a rich elder and asks him to undertake the marriage insurance payments to the family of his chosen bride. In return the poor man binds himself to the rich man as a serf. It often happens that the old man comes to look upon his serf as an adopted son, or even as his heir.

A few marriages are based upon child betrothals,

especially among the Nilotic peoples and also among some Bantu groups. The betrothal of infant girls is legal and the custom appears to be very ancient. Parents of a little girl who accept her betrothal to a man are expected to bring her up in the knowledge that she will marry him in due course. After the age of six or seven, a betrothed girl often goes to live with her future husband's family. If the girl, when grown to marriageable age, decides that she does not after all wish to marry her betrothed there are ways by which she can escape the obligation. But it is usually a costly procedure for her parents to get out of the arrangement. In fact betrothal has become less and less widespread, but still sometimes occurs.

Among some African tribes, although marriage to a blood relation has normally been taboo and considered incestuous, it was nevertheless required of members of a ruling house. For example in Uganda a prince of the royal house was expected to marry his sister or at least a close family cousin who, by tribal law, also ranked as a sister. It is hard to say whether marriages of brothers and sisters and close cousins were in fact ever more than legal marriages. Although anthropologists who have described brother/sister marriages have usually assumed that they did include sexual intercourse, the horror of incest among all tribes makes it unlikely that they were consummated.

Only when a marriage has completely broken down because of one partner's refusal to accept responsibility for children is dissolution or divorce ever anything but extremely difficult. Divorce or dissolution has always however been allowed. When marriages are childless for several years, the bride's family hands back the same number of stock as was handed over originally at the time of her marriage, but not in this case the computed offspring. When a man whose marriage has failed to produce any children realises that the fault is possibly his, rather than his wife's, he tends to encourage her to sleep with other men and try to produce a family for him. In the rare event of legal divorce or dissolution of marriage the status of the children depends entirely on the decision of the elders. In most tribes, at least before Christian influence, married men and women have had considerable sexual freedom, always provided that they do not conceal their love affairs from the other party. Concealment makes them liable to a charge of adultery.

Both men and women in most tribes can in various easy ways legally break off all sexual relationships with their marriage partner. For example if a Kikuyu married woman wants to stop sleeping with her husband, all she has to do is find a moment when he is in the compound in daylight, take off all her clothes and appear before him naked. From this moment on it is illegal for these two ever to have sexual relations together again, although of course the husband retains responsibility for his children.

Muslims may, as laid down in the Koran, marry up to four legal wives. Their wives are often closely guarded and forbidden to have any physical relationship with other men. Should they transgress they risk being divorced and being deprived of a guardian unless they manage to marry again. Muslim women, who have usually been brought up strictly, are not usually promiscuous. They live in fear that their husbands will divorce them at a whim, leaving them destitute. In most Muslim communities, a man can legally divorce his wife just by saying to her slowly three times in the presence of a witness 'I divorce you'. The woman's safeguard has lain in the fact that such a statement is not a valid divorce if she has one foot or both feet in water. So married Muslim women who are afraid their husbands might divorce them have traditionally often kept a bowl of water handy.

Almost from the beginning of the introduction of Christianity to the peoples of Africa, Christian converts began to question the teachings of their respective churches on the alleged wickedness of polygamy. They were and are avid readers of the vernacular translations of both Old and New Testaments, and have been quick to realize that nowhere has Christ said anything about polygamy; moreover the New Testament suggests that those who are not bishops, priests or deacons could be practising Christians and yet be husbands of more than one wife. One of the major results of this disagreement between Christianity, as taught by the missionaries, and Christianity as interpreted by the Africans themselves has been the establishment of many breakaway Christian Churches which mainly differ from orthodox Christianity by allowing polygamy.

Peoples of southern Africa

Southern Africa is a sub-continent of vivid anthropological contrasts: from the small Bushman band, with a rudimentary technology and simple hunting and gathering economy, to the large urban population of Johannesburg, clustered around a wealthy, technologically advanced mining and industrial complex; from black tribesmen who cling to traditional life-styles in their rural territories, to the urban African populations who have adapted to an urban culture. Southern Africa's peoples include swampland fishing tribes using primitive craft, and wealthy mechanized maize and stock farmers; tribal pastoralists constantly beset by drought; affluent merchants and industrialists.

In western Botswana and South-west Africa lies the Kalahari Desert. Here Bushmen eke out a meager existence in the barren, sandy wasteland. Not far to the north, in Ngamiland (northern Botswana), the lush Okavango swampland supports indigenous sedentary village populations, a considerable game population and a thriving international safari industry. In contrast, the Karoo region of the Cape, in the heartland of South Africa, is a high, arid, infertile belt in which only sheep can really thrive—while some two hundred miles away, in the Mediterranean climate of the southern Cape, wine and fruit farms flourish. Over relatively short distances, there are dramatic ecological contrasts.

Historically, too, southern Africa is the homeland of a polyglot population of many different origins. Accumulating archaeological evidence suggests the existence of iron-working people in Swaziland as early as the 5th century. But many of the modern southern African chiefdoms are believed to have had their origins in the area of Africa's great lakes and to have migrated southwards several centuries ago—though dating their movements is difficult. Some of these chiefdoms have mythologies which allude to the migration, but an oral history does not necessarily provide accurate historical data. Indeed the pre-18th century history of southern Africa is still unclear. Early in the 19th century a period of turbulent wars set the tribes of the sub-continent in motion. The Zulu, under Shaka (1816-28), initiated a vast series of military campaigns which, in turn, stimulated further belligerence on the part of the famous Matabele warrior-chief, Mzilikaze, whose people established themselves in what is now Rhodesia. The effect of these wars was felt throughout southern Africa. The populations of many chiefdoms were decimated; others were put to flight and forced to seek out new territory.

Until this time, contact between black Africans and white settlers from Europe had been largely restricted to a few missionaries and travelers who had ventured inland – it was only in the coastal regions that the two peoples were in regular contact. But in the 1830s groups of colonists, mainly of Dutch descent, began to make their way inland. In search of fresh farmland and a desire to rid themselves of the oppressive colonial administration, the Boer farmers of the Great Trek gradually established themselves in the southern African hinterland. The Boers' descendants were to form the Afrikaner population of the sub-continent.

The Cape Colony, from which the Boers emigrated, had by this time become a thriving place with its capital at Cape Town. Since Jan van Riebeeck of the Dutch East India Company first established a station at the Cape in 1652, it had been administered first by the Dutch and then the British, and had gradually absorbed divers settler populations from England, Holland, Germany and France. The British, however, did not succeed in turning the Dutch Afrikaners into loyal subjects of the Crown. Indeed the 19th century conflict between the English and the Dutch speaking colonists constituted a *leitmotif* in the development of the growing community. The Great Trek was one of the earliest expressions of this conflict – and it brought the Boers into contact with the black chiefdoms of the interior. What followed was a protracted series of military and diplomatic battles in which every side sought to secure its own future. And although, in 1910, South Africa became an independent Union, the Boer, British and African peoples continued to assert their separate identities. Out of these conflicts also came the three former British High Commission territories (now Botswana, Lesotho and Swaziland) as Britain extended her protection to the native inhabitants of those areas. The creation of Rhodesia as a settler colony also followed on events in South Africa – although in this case there were the additional ambitions of the British South Africa Company and particularly Cecil John Rhodes.

This historical process did not, however, extend to the other territories of southern Africa. South-west Africa (Namibia) was originally colonized by Germany, then lost to the Allies in World War I, and is now a mandated territory of South Africa. Angola and Mozambique, on whose coasts the Portuguese had been established since the 15th and 16th centuries, came under Portuguese control following the late 19th century 'scramble for Africa'; and there they have remained. But the League of Nations, which mandated formerly German South-west Africa to South Africa after the first world war is gone; South Africa's right to rule in South-west Africa is being disputed by black-ruled African states. The status of Rhodesia, too, is also challenged as a result of her unilateral declaration of independence from Britain. African movements are at work in Mozambique and Angola to free these countries of Portuguese colonialism. The political independence of Botswana, Lesotho and Swaziland does not give them economic independence. And the future map of South Africa envisaged by her present government is planned to comprise a number of ethnic lands, so-called 'Bantustans' such as the Xhosa territory of the Transkei and Ciskei, possibly bound together in a multi-national state.

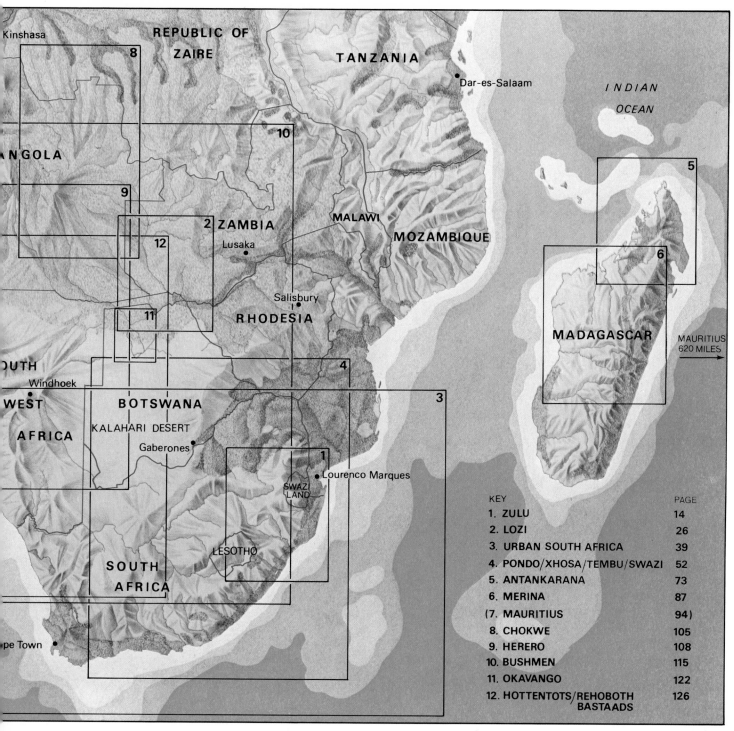

KEY	PAGE
1. ZULU	14
2. LOZI	26
3. URBAN SOUTH AFRICA	39
4. PONDO/XHOSA/TEMBU/SWAZI	52
5. ANTANKARANA	73
6. MERINA	87
(7. MAURITIUS	94)
8. CHOKWE	105
9. HERERO	108
10. BUSHMEN	115
11. OKAVANGO	122
12. HOTTENTOTS/REHOBOTH BASTAADS	126

The contrasts and diversities of geography and history apply equally to the societies and cultures of southern Africa. This dimension has been left aside, as the various contributions will present the reader with a sample of different life-styles. But this volume cannot present an exhaustive survey of all the peoples of this region of the world – that would be a mammoth task. Rather, it sets out to present some of the social and cultural variations, and some of the similarities. The chapters on the Zulu (pages 14-25), Swazi, Pondo, Xhosa and Tembu (pages 52-59) give a broad view of the Bantu-speaking Nguni peoples of southern Africa. The people of the Okavango (pages 122-125) illustrate the south-western Bantu people on the verge of the Kalahari desert where Bushmen survive with their singular and ancient adaptation to so harsh an environment. The chapters on the Lozi (pages 26-29) and the Chokwe (pages 104-107) expand the geographical spectrum to include Zambia and Angola. Then, by way of contrast, the Afrikaners who constitute one influential sector of the white community are described (pages 62-65). Finally, a chapter on mining is included (pages 46-51). This is appropriate in a volume concerning a region where industry is one of the major arenas of inter-community contact, and of social change.

13

Zulus
South Africa

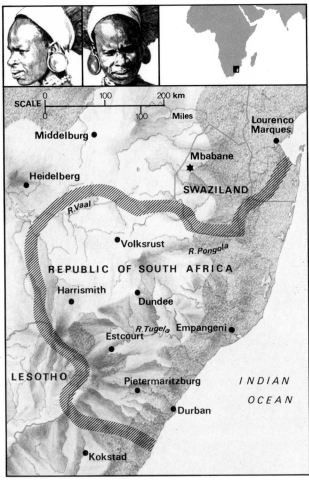

SCALE
0   100   200 km
0   100   Miles

Middelburg ●

Heidelberg ●

SWAZILAND

★ Mbabane

Lourenco Marques

R.Vaal

Volksrust ●

R.Pongola

REPUBLIC OF SOUTH AFRICA

Harrismith ●

Dundee ●

R.Tugela   Empangeni ●

Estcourt ●

LESOTHO

Pietermaritzburg ●

INDIAN OCEAN

● Durban

● Kokstad

No one knows how long people have lived in the southern part of the African continent. Experts date signs of iron work in Swaziland as 5th century. Seamen wrecked on the east coat of South Africa in the 16th century contacted cattle keepers and farmers there. When later, Europeans came in force to South Africa, they found on the east coast of Natal a people who called themselves *A ma Zulu.*

Nathaniel Isaacs lived among the Zulu in the region of the great monarch Shaka. 'The Zoola men' he said 'are without exception the finest race of people that I have ever seen . . . They are tall, athletic, well-proportioned and good featured . . . capable of enduring great fatigue, both in war and in hunting excursions, and their agility is almost beyond comprehension.' It was under Shaka's rule, from 1816–1828, that the Zulu nation reached the zenith of its power. Through his well disciplined, highly trained army he united the clusters of people who belonged to independent chiefdoms into a single nation.

Shaka divided his troops by age into regiments and quartered them for most of the year in large barracks in different parts of the country where they trained and, when not at war, herded cattle and worked in the fields.

14

15

Zulus liken women to the soil:
they are the channel through
which life enters the world
and through which it leaves,
for only women mourn the dead.

Zulus South Africa

An artist depicts Cetshwayo's army of 40,000 charging the British lines during the Zulu war of 1897 which crushed Zulu power for ever.

Shaka revolutionized his army's fighting power by introducing a short stabbing *assegai* for use in hand to hand fighting – an innovation which put the old courtly method of fighting with the throwing *assegai* out of date – and by assembling the army in mass attack formations and enclosing the enemy in a half moon until it was completely surrounded. Any enemy warriors who survived the onslaught were incorporated into the Zulu army. After Shaka was assassinated in 1828 the power of the Zulu was to decline. His half brother and successor Dingane was as tyrannous, though not as successful a ruler as Shaka, and soon the people transferred their allegiance from him to his brother Mpande who, with the help of white settlers (by now firmly entrenched in Natal), defeated, ousted and succeeded Dingane. It was during the reign of Mpande's successor – his son Cetshwayo – that in 1879 the Zulu nation was defeated, Cetshwayo was deposed and relegated to paramount chief, and the nation divided into 13 kingdoms.

Today the Zulu kingdom is stripped of all effective power and ostensibly the Zulu, who are today well over four million strong are simply the largest of the cultural groups into which South Africa is divided by its apartheid policy. But the people regard themselves as one nation in culture, language, ambitions and leadership. A Zulu nation dwells on in their minds. And, although the kingdom is lost, even in the modern form of elected government in the framework of South African politics Zulu leaders are often closely associated with Shaka's royal line. The elected leader of the Kwa-Zulu Territorial government is Gatsha Mangosuthu Buthelezi, a university graduate who is traditional leader of the Buthelezi, one of the leading chiefdoms, and whose mother is a daughter of the late paramount chief Dinizulu and a full sister of the late paramount chief Nkayishana. The present paramount chief, Buthelezi's cousin, is Zwelithini (Goodwill), son of Nkayishana.

The paramount chief's power now largely derives from the fact that he represents the great tradition of the Zulu kings and, as such, is a symbol of Zulu nationalism. Chiefs too have a stronger position among their people as representatives of the paramount chief than as the nominated representatives of the white government, although today their actual governmental power is circumscribed by the system by which the Zulu are divided into a number of magisterial districts, in turn subdivided into areas ruled by hereditary chiefs who only have a limited amount of judicial authority, and must assist the European in administration. The magistrate not only applies government regulations, he is also the local representative of the many changes the government has made in the lives of the Zulu: the establishment of health, veterinary and agricultural services, the building of schools and the provision of labor for European farms and industries. The magistrate has to do many things which the chief can no longer do through lack of power

Mine dancing was started for
workers to 'let off steam';
it is now a tourist attraction
with troupes like this one in
Johannesburg, touring cities.

Zulus South Africa

By the time Ntshingwayo became chief in 1895 the Zulu state had been broken up into powerless chiefdoms under white rule.

Dinizulu's aunt, 'queen' of Zululand in the 1890s. Her bride-price would have been at least twenty *ilobolo* cattle.

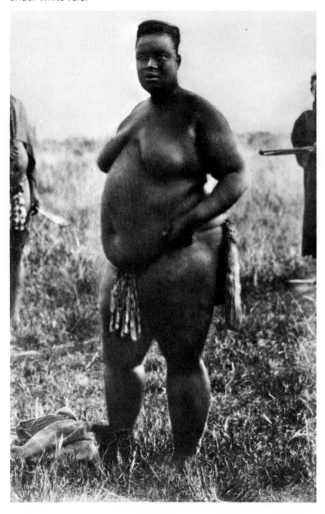

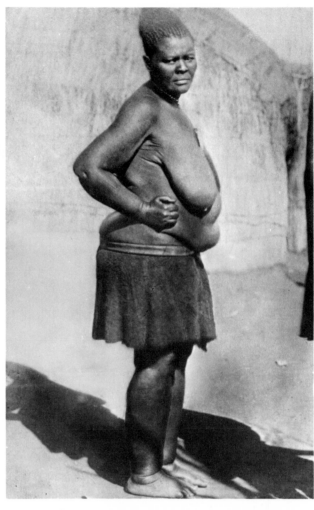

and knowledge. It is he and not the chief who is in a position to do most to help the Zulu to adapt to the changes which are being imposed on their old way of life. There is often conflict between chiefs and magistrate.

To keep their valued tradition and identity alive the Zulu have much to contend with. Shortage of land and the exigencies of the western life-style have disturbed the old way of life based on cattle raising and agriculture and have brought them much deprivation. Many now live in townships near the mines and cities where they work; others are laborers on white-owned farms. Families have been split up as the men tend to be away most of the time, returning to their homes only weekly or monthly. Christianity, too, has had an erosive cultural effect, for it has disturbed the ancestral cult, a corner-stone of Zulu culture.

Zulu society has lost much of its stability, for not only are changes being made with increasing speed, but also the different authorities stand for contradictory values. Ultimate power rests with the European government against which the chief can do little. Even so, the smaller

groups in Zulu society, the clans and the homesteads, have remained relatively constant and many Zulu are still determined to uphold their culture and to preserve their heritage through traditional institutions.

Zulu are traditionally polygamous, living in homesteads – circles of grass-thatched huts, usually surrounded by hedges dotted along ridges and valleys. One or possibly two of these huts – one for sleeping in, the other for daily chores – is occupied by each wife. The senior wife's hut stands by the entrance near the cattle fold. Each woman has not only her own hut, but also her own granary and her own fields. For grown-up children there is one hut for the youths, another for the girls.

But as less free land is available for pasture and farming, and the women are left to till the fields alone to supplement the men's wages, and, as most marriages are anyway now monogamous, homesteads like these are decreasing. The homesteads splinter into smaller units. The men leave to seek work in the towns as migrant labor.

The circular shape of the traditional homestead has a deep symbolic meaning. The round hut is the womb, and

Although the office of paramount chief means little real power, 25,000 Zulu attended the installation of 23-year-old Zwelithini.

Zululand now has its own parliament. Many of the elected representatives, here arriving for a session, are also hereditary chiefs.

the Zulu say of a woman's children 'they are of the same hut – the same womb'. Graves too are circular, with a niche in the side. The corpse is buried in a sitting position in the niche, a foetus ready to be born into the other world. The entire extended family of the homestead is dominated by the notion of sharing. The main meal of the day is provided, cooked and served by all the wives at about 2 pm. They each divide their contribution to the meal into three dishes – one for the men, one for the women and one for the children – which they carry over to the main hut of the senior wife where the meal is served. Inside men sit on the right and women on the left. If there are six married women, each of whom has done her share of the cooking, there will be six different kinds of food for each of the three groups of men, women and children. Each group eats from one dish at a time, taking their share and then passing it on until it is all finished. At this meal not only is every member of the homestead well fed; it is a social occasion during which people relax and chat, and adults are conscious of teaching children etiquette. They watch carefully how the children take their share from the dish, for eating from one dish stresses the value of sharing. The morning and evening meals are not communal. Each woman serves her own husband and children a lighter meal of snacks, leftovers or curdled milk food.

The importance of sharing is taken well beyond meal times in the senior wife's hut. The Zulu place particular value on cattle, their chief traditional source of wealth. But the exigencies of sharing are stronger. Any member of the homestead may take milk from a cow whenever he wishes. And there is a custom of sharing milk outside the homestead, known as *ukusisa*, by which a man will often give one of his milk cows into the care of a neighbor who does not have any cows in milk, until the neighbor is able to supply his family with milk from his own cows. Kings and chiefs have always made extensive use of this system. By loaning out his cattle to his people to herd for him the chief provided them with milk and meat, and as a by-product increased their dependence and allegiance to him. If he wished he could inflict great hardship by taking away his cattle. Only recently a certain chief had 16,000 cattle out of a tribal total of 54,000 loaned out among his people. This custom is central to Zulu society even today. Crops too are shared in time of need. The Zulu rarely store or sell their crops. If the maize, beans, colocasia, sweet and plain potatoes, groundnuts, sorghum 19 and pumpkins with tender leaves eaten as spinach, which they cultivate, should fail neighboring homesteads will share what they have. The Zulu hold it a disgrace to eat while a neighbor starves. This they say is 'the behavior of animals, not humans'.

In spring when the harvest is exhausted they depend heavily on the men's wages, but in summer when there is plenty of fresh green food, they spend their wages on building new houses, on clothes or household equipment.

If a man leaves the homestead for the town, or if he lets land remain unused, the chief of the territorial unit in which he lives also acts as main arbitrator in all disputes over land and can take it over and put it to better use. Land is owned collectively. Individuals have no freehold rights to it but instead have rights of use over the land they farm as members of the chiefdom. Pasture land is common to all. People are free to collect dry wood and herbal medicines from the bush, but they may not cut down trees without the chief's permission. Anyone can use the strips in between fields and the fields lying fallow for grazing cattle. When the harvest is over cattle may graze anywhere.

Newcomers may settle within a chiefdom provided a resident will vouch for them. The new family live with their sponsor for as long as the other residents take to decide if they are acceptable. Then, in the presence of the chief or his representative, the sponsor sets aside a piece of his own land for his friend. The residents must now voice any objections they have against the newcomer, and take careful note of the boundaries. Once he has been 'placed' and has paid a small fee to the chief, the newcomer is not only a paid-up but a fully participating member of the chiefdom.

Heads of homesteads and their dependents like to trace descent from a common great grandfather and can always turn to each other in times of need. Members of one lineage, traced back to a common grandfather, have even greater religious and social obligations towards each other. They jointly carry out religious practices, jointly make sacrifices and may not work sorcery against each other, nor quarrel – if they do they must perform a rite to appease their ancestors and make good their differences. Descendants of a common grandfather live in separate homesteads, but form a territorial unit. The lineage leader, the senior male, holds the lineage land in trust for his kinsmen and may not dispose of it without their consent. He also holds a court which settles disputes within the lineage. The ancestors sanction the behavior of members of the same lineage and have much more influence on daily life than do the supreme beings – the First Being and the Princess of the Sky.

In the beginning there was the First Being, followed by the Princess of the Sky; later, a reed growing on the river bank burgeoned and gave birth to man. The people multiplied and the First Being sent a chameleon to tell them they should not die. Then he sent a lizard to tell the people that they would die. The lizard overtook the chameleon which had stopped along the way to eat some wild red berries. When the chameleon arrived last and delivered his message 'the people shall not die', they refused to believe him and instead decided to stick to the first message brought by the lizard. And so the people began to die. But then the Princess of the Sky made the people, the animals and the land fertile. Ever since, every spring married women and maidens perform rites to the Princess to ensure a good crop, more cattle and healthy babies. The Zulu approach the First Being only when a catastrophe, like extreme drought, is near. Then both men and women join in the ritual. Otherwise the First Being and the Princess live 'above' and do not affect day-to-day life.

The ancestors, on the other hand, the spirits of the dead who live 'below' are always close to their people. When things go well the Zulu say 'the ancestors are with us', but when they suffer misfortune they say 'the ancestors are facing away from us'. After the appropriate rites have been performed dead spirits return to this world as invisible members of society. The spirits of the mother, the father and both the father's parents have power to bless and punish. The head of the homestead contacts the ancestors whose main concern is for the welfare of their descendants, by making sacrifices for himself and for his dependents. A person sins against the ancestors when he transgresses in his duties to members of his lineage or against the rules of marriage.

When a man marries the Zulu say, he 'takes the wife'. When a woman marries she 'travels on a long journey' not only because physically she joins her husband in his home, but because although of a different lineage to her husband, she becomes a wife and mother to his lineage. Her own ancestors protect her as a daughter, her husband's ancestors guard her as a wife and mother. Gradually she is assimilated into her husband's lineage until by the time she reaches the menopause she ceases to observe the rites and taboos of her original lineage. Finally when she dies she becomes an ancestral spirit as a mother, not as a daughter, lives with her husband's family spirits and returns to the world through sacrifices made by her husband's group.

Before a marriage both families negotiate. The man's family takes the initiative and of the gifts that are subsequently exchanged the cattle given by the man's family are the most important. They are *ilobolo* cattle, ten for the girl's father, the eleventh for her mother. This mother's cow is a gift which cannot be returned, even if the marriage breaks up. If it is a chief's or a headman's daughter who is getting married more cattle are required. Usually 20 animals are given to a chief and 15 to a headman. The bride's father has the duty of performing rites and sacrificing cattle to make his daughter fertile. The *ilobolo* cattle in fact are the means by which the bridegroom aquires legal rights over his future children.

The Zulu say 'cattle beget children' and 'the children are where the cattle are not'.

Children belong to their father's lineage. Zulu society is patrilineal, an order of things explained in the Zulu mind by the analogy of sowing a seed. The child belongs to the man, the farmer who has sown the seed. If the marriage breaks up, then he keeps the children. The woman is likened to the soil, through which new life enters the world. If her husband dies she remains a member of her husband's group and if still fertile will continue to bear children for the group by her husband's younger brother. These children belong not to the brother but to the dead husband. This arrangement does not interfere with the brother's own family. He merely helps to provide for the widow and her children.

When girls reach puberty they are organized into territorial age-sets, each with the eldest girl as leader, whose duty it is to instruct the others in sex. A girl may accept a suitor without first telling the leader, who must then organize a special ceremony. She appoints a day when the young man, accompanied by his age-mates, is invited to be publicly decorated with beads by the girls. This is entirely the affair of the young people of the area. Adults take no part in it and appear to know nothing about it. The girl must preserve her virginity until marriage, so although premarital sexual contacts are allowed, they are strictly controlled; full sexual intercourse is forbidden. The young man and the girl are both instructed in *ukusoma,* external intercourse, by their age-mates.

A girl who loses her virginity or becomes pregnant before marriage disgraces all the other girls in her group. They demand a goat from the young man responsible, with which they may perform a cleansing ritual. The pregnant girl then drops out of her age-group and may not associate with it. The man must pay a fine to the chief, an ox to the girl's father and a cow to her mother. In most cases the young man would open marriage negotiations as soon as the girl became pregnant. If the girl later marries someone else her father may accept only nine cattle and her mother will not be given her cow. The girl's parents will adopt the baby when it is born by performing a sacrifice to thank the ancestors for its safe delivery, to explain how it was born and to ask them to protect the baby as one of their own. The young mother then takes on the status of the baby's sister. The Zulu have no circumcision or initiation rites, but girls perform nubility rites to make them fertile as soon as they reach marriageable age.

The Zulu recognize two distinct types of illness. Diseases, colds and epidemics they realize, happen not through any malicious outside interference and can be cured by medicines. But the causes of the second type of illness are found only in Zulu cosmology. Sickness is often the result of sorcery, the wrath of an ancestor, pollution or a 'disordered' state of mind. Sorcery works along social lines. Heads of homesteads, who alone can contact the ancestors and invoke them to abandon another member of the same lineage group, have the power to practise sorcery and thus the power to affect a man in every aspect of his life: his crops, his cattle, his health. Sorcery is often practised at night. An evil-hearted, envious sorcerer may harm others by visiting their homesteads at night and scattering dangerous substances which harm all the inhabitants including the animals. As only men may travel about freely at night, women can never become night sorcerers although they do practise sorcery on a smaller scale, harming only individuals they dislike, usually by poisoning their food.

While men always work their sorcery consciously, through malice, all women are thought to be polluted at certain times: during menstruation, lactation and during and after pregnancy. This pollution is a mystical force believed to lower the woman's resistance to disease, make her accident prone, disagreeable and even repulsive to others. The pollution when it is at its worst, just after birth, is contagious and particularly dangerous to men's virility. In this crucial period the new mother must withdraw from society as she may pick up diseases and pass them on to her child. She must also avoid all men and cattle. She must avoid growing crops and eat no milk food. A menstruating woman is less contagious, but nevertheless so polluting as to be a threat to the virility of men and the well-being of cattle and crops. Death also pollutes. Pollution emanates from the corpse as well as the chief mourner who is always a married woman. The highest point of contagious pollution is during the time between death and burial. Until the burial the chief mourner must sit alone with the corpse, accompanied only by other married women, just as at birth she is alone with the baby and other women. Birth and death are parallel, and women are the symbolic channel of arrival into this world and departure to the next. Even female ancestral spirits are believed to be capricious and evil and will continue to send misfortune even after the correct rites and sacrifices have been performed. Male ancestral spirits on the other hand, send misfortune only where it is deserved and lift it after sacrifice. Dangerous forked lightning is female, sheet lightning is male.

A man who kills another is polluted, no matter whether he killed accidentally, in self-defense, in war or in cold blood, or whether he killed a stranger or a kinsman. Once he has taken human life a man has assumed the woman's role and, like the chief mourner, is polluted and must withdraw from society. While it is immoral to practise sorcery, to be polluted is not in itself immoral. But to flout the correct forms of behavior when polluted is indeed immoral.

The Zulu believe in a special, delicately balanced relationship between man and his surroundings which can be affected by plant and animal life. Men and animals leave something of themselves behind when they 21

move on, and absorb into themselves something of the atmosphere into which they move. When a Zulu enters an area markedly different from his home region he is likely to be ill. And when he returns, both men and animals bring with them foreign elements which may pollute their home region. The countryside is further polluted if an illness is removed from the human system and thrown away. What is discarded is dangerous for it does not dissipate, but hovers around the place where it was thrown. Night sorcerers make the world an even more dangerous place by scattering the paths with evil substances to harm passers-by. As the environment is so riddled with dangers medical treatment is not only for the sick. People take treatment from time to time just to sustain their resistance.

Most traditional medicines are herbal, although some come from animals. Doctors are usually men, and serve an apprenticeship, although sometimes they are diviners, possessed by the ancestral spirits who endow them with clairvoyance, when they are normally women – male diviners become transvestites. The diviner eventually acquires as wide a knowledge of medicine as the doctor.

The Zulu suffer in the conflict between Zulu and western culture. In their society, moderation is the rule. A man must have neither too much nor too little of the desired things of life, and must share both food and good fortune. Even during the zenith of Zulu power these principles were evident. Shaka the conqueror subdued but never enslaved. Nobles and commoners alike ate the same food and obeyed the same laws. The imposition of white rule with its capitalist competitive values conflicts not only with Zulu notions of striking a balance but also with the idea of corporate responsibility within the homestead. The Zulu have been forced to adapt to values which are entirely contradictory to their own traditions. Even so, their own culture does prevail and despite all the stresses, provides the Zulu people with deep and satisfying answers.

1	4	
2	5	7
3	6	

4 By wearing Edwardian dress, the defeated nation's leaders tried to adopt the styles of their new masters after the last revolt of 1907.

1 Homesteads like these in Natal are declining as monogamy and migrant labor upset traditional clan and family relationships.

2 Courting clothes include everything bought while working in the mines or the city as well as the traditional red and white courting cloth.

3 Today some Zulu women wear traditional dress for the benefit of tourists who will pay to be allowed to photograph them.

5 Missionaries and colonists followed close upon each other —Wesleyan hymns instilled a sense of sin, high-necked dresses concealed shame.

6 The status of witchdoctors has diminished but they remain an important part of tribal life with the power to cast spells and inspire fear.

7 Western culture has intruded upon the traditional puberty ceremony. Now women dance carrying purses and other finery purchased in the city.

(Over page) Young unmarried girls line up to perform the python dance, a kind of 'conga' which has variations all over Africa.

23

83159

Lozi
Zambia

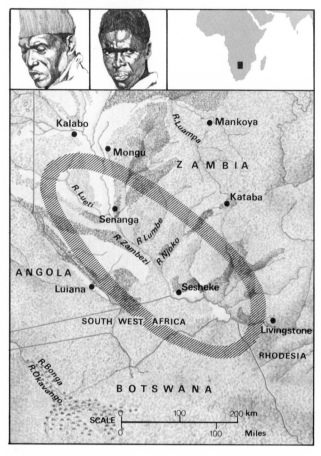

From December to April every year the home of the Lozi is submerged in the flood waters of the Upper Zambezi. The great meandering river drives the plain dwellers into their other homes on higher land. Even the snakes and the warrior ants follow processions of cattle out of the river's path, and most people take to canoes. The Zambezi brings with it wealth in many forms: all kinds of fish, transport, natural irrigation, and woods providing game and fruit, and when it subsides it leaves behind fertility in the silt, giving rich grazing for cattle and land ready for growing maize and millet. The Zambezi has been bringing the Lozi its great yearly tribute for centuries.

The Lozi say that God married his own daughter and had many sons. One of these princes was walking one day in the lands of the Lozi, and passed a fishing party by a pool. The fishermen, who were men of two western tribes, were also visitors. Out of respect for the son of God they offered him some of their fish. Lozi onlookers were also impressed by this prince, and asked the daughter of God if she would give him one of her sons to be the king. She gave them this very prince, her eldest son, to be their king. This myth describes not only the beginning of the Lozi kingdom, but also the tribute system on which their economy has been based.

Until the 20th century when they lost dominion over many of their lands the Lozi (Malozi or Barotse, as they are alternatively called) dominated a vast area which now covers a large part of western Zambia, parts of Southern Rhodesia, the Caprivi strip of South-west Africa, and eastern Angola. But in the beginning – when they were called Aluyi – they absorbed and conquered many peoples in all directions, mainly east and south, including the two unrelated tribes of the fishermen of the old myth, who were willing subjects. In the 19th and 20th centuries groups of Mbunda entered the kingdom as migrants from the west, with Lubale and related villagers. At its largest the Lozi kingdom must have been at least forty thousand square miles and inhabited by about two hundred thousand people.

The Lozi's rich, varied, economically complex homeland is in the flood plain of the Upper Zambezi, which has been carved by the meanderings of the great river – 25 miles across at its widest – as it cut its way from north to south towards the wind-blown sand of Kalahari. It is bounded by bushed scarps which give way to woodlands interspersed with small circular plains with wet, grassy or marshy centers, and with small lakes and tributaries. The plain itself is full of former ox-bows (lakes formed by old river paths). These are the home of many kinds of fish and wild-fowl, crocodiles and hippopotamuses. In December almost every year the plain floods with the rains that fall on the divides between the Zambezi and the Congo, Kafue and Kwando rivers. By February or March the plain has usually become a vast lake. The Lozi cultivated plots on the plain, on higher land enriched by termites and the droppings of cattle staked there. Their plots in lower parts of the plain were enriched with the silt and underground seepage. The land along the margins of the plain, drained by large canals dug by kings and fed by smaller channels dug by landowners, also drew on underground water. The land in the bounding woodlands was dependent on the summer rains. A Northern Rhodesian Government ecological survey said that the Lozi made such efficient use of their arable resources that no improvements could be suggested. They grew maize, sorghum and millet; sweetreed, Livingstone and sweet potatoes, and later American fruits and vegetables brought in the 19th century by the Christian missionaries. When the plain was not flooded it provided rich grazing for cattle and in the past, before they were shot out, vast herds of antelope. The Lozi had much milk and meat, cattle, game and wildfowl, as well as domestic fowl. They drew also a rich harvest of fish, caught by 23 different methods according to the movement of the fish with the rise and fall of the river.

To exploit these varied resources the Lozi built different homes for different seasons. In dry periods they lived in the marshy plains on raised land, some of which the kings raised artificially to form islands. When

26

The rise and fall of the
Zambezi dominates life. The
Lozi have 23 different ways
of catching fish, and a
barbed spear for crocodiles.

the flood rose, the people abandoned these homes with their cattle and moved to homes built on the margins of the plain.

This movement, and the combination of agriculture, herding cattle, fishing and hunting, working woods, reeds and ironstone, and collecting honey and wild fruit, meant that the Lozi had simultaneously to perform productive tasks all over a vast area of land.

Each Lozi village was a corporate group which controlled the land and fishing sites attached to it. Some villages were royal or attached to councillors' titles; other villages were owned by extended families. The king had power to move people from village to village and arrange co-operation. The people themselves fostered joint enterprise; they were interested in linking many villages and families by marriage. Only the royal family had one line of descent; the system for everyone else was omnilineal, forbidding marriage between people who had even a great-great-grand parent in common: fourth cousins were not allowed to marry. Divorce was common, possibly because everyone moved around so much. Lozi relationships were widespread.

The Lozi were always short of labor and this perhaps is why Lozi kings refused to allow the slavers to get slaves from among their subjects and serfs. The kings also kept bringing in *maketo* (chosen people) from distant provinces to settle royal villages in the plains. The withdrawal of labor from this complex economy when men went to work for European enterprises hit it more severely than it hit less complex indigenous economies.

In 1838, soon after a civil war, the Lozi were conquered by the Kololo, a Sotho group which was fleeing from Lesotho (Basutoland). Some Lozi princes fled north and established three small kingdoms. Most of their followers were Mbunda, and gradually the few Lozi exiles became Mbunda-ized. A different, bigger group of Lozi, including many princes, stayed under Kololo rule. These were the people visited by David Livingstone in 1853-54 and 1860-61; they financed and staffed his great crossing of Africa. This entire group spoke Kololo, a Sotho language – though it has many words of Aluyi origin. One of the Lozi princes eventually fled from this group, and went north to one of the kingdoms in exile, and in 1864 came back to annihilate the Kololo, and re-established the Luyi (Lozi) dynasty. After a period of civil wars his grandson regained the throne – with the support of the people in the south – conquered the northern kingdoms and actually increased the extent of Lozi rule. He died in 1916.

In 1900 the Lozi sought British protection through the British South Africa Company, and abandoned land to Germany and the British ruled territories of Bechuanaland and Southern Rhodesia. Within the British protectorate of Northern Rhodesia, they had a special treaty relationship which reserved many privileges for them. Although they lost their suzerainty there over the Totela, Toka, Ila and Kaonde peoples in the east, in the north they were granted control over Balovale district (Zambia), but lost this in 1941 after trying to set up an unpopular Lozi capital there.

The Barotse, or Lozi, were one of the largest traditional states and played an important role through the period of colonial rule into African independence for Zambia. But they have declined in importance. When Livingstone visited Loziland in 1854-55, after traveling through Tswana country and then up the Zambezi, he lyrically compared the Zambezi flood-plain to the Land of Canaan flowing with milk and honey. He and later observers witnessed the influx of tribute to the capitals from all corners of the nation and being redistributed by the rulers among their subjects. It was little changed by as late as the 1940s.

With the development of the modern economy of Zambia along the rail line from Livingstone to the copper mines of Zambia and Zaïre, Barotseland became an isolated region. To earn the money needed to pay taxes, and to purchase European goods, the Lozi export the labor of their able-bodied young men to white towns and industries as far south as South Africa. Without their labor, home production has deteriorated seriously. Later with more births and immigrants, the Lozi over-cultivated and two serious attacks of bovine pleuro-pneumonia depleted their herds. The land of milk and honey is now impoverished.

The king and the royal family have always been closely

The Lozi say their king, here borne on the royal barge, is God's grandson. When he dies the nation and the earth 'fall into a deep coma'.

For four months every year the Lozi's homeland is submerged by the flooding Zambezi. Families take to their dugout canoes.

identified with the natural forces so important to the Lozi. The king is Mbumu-wa-Litunga, 'Great one of the earth'. It is believed that when the king dies, the nation and the earth fall into a coma. All fires are put out and relit when the new king is installed with fire from the shrine of the Daughter-of-God. To the south of the royal capital is another capital of lesser importance ruled through most of Lozi history by a sister, aunt or daughter of the reigning king, known as *Litunga-la-Mooela*, 'Earth-of-the-South'. Although the northern capital was more powerful, its decisions had to receive the sanction of the southern one. In ritual terms, the identification of the kings with the Earth was marked also by the cenotaphs of dead kings, groves planted at their graves on large islands in the flood plain at which national offerings were regularly made at the great national ceremonies, when the Earths – or rulers – led their people out of the plain to the margins and back, with national and royal bands playing in great fleets of barges and canoes.

Christianity came to the Lozi in the late 1880s. Members of the Paris Evangelical Mission from Basutoland met some Lozi refugees from the civil wars who persuaded them to go to the Lozi. The king finally agreed to the mission. This decision was crucial to the future history of the Barotse nation. The missionaries persuaded the king to accept British rather than French or German protection. They also wrote the Lozi language, trans-

lated the Bible, recorded their history, and set up schools. The missionaries induced the king to abandon his raids on other people.

The king governed through a complex series of councils. On the right of the throne sat councillors, whose titles represented the rights of the nation in the kingdom. On the left sat stewards who looked after the king's household affairs and represented the rights of the reigning king. In front sat princes and husbands of princesses, who represented the rights of the royal family. The full council was divided down the middle into senior and junior sets reaching across all three blocks; when there were important issues to debate, the two were equal. In addition, the king was advised by favored councillors at secret nocturnal meetings, a princess and a commoner woman, who were here especially appointed, to eavesdrop on these meetings and to give the king advice, and with their womanly compassion, restrain him from harsh counsels which might alienate his people. His rule was centralized avoiding local factions and the growth of private armies. This organization worked with restricted powers under the British, but on a territorial division of the country. Since Zambian independence in 1964 the power of the traditional authorities has been yet more severely curtailed. In the 20th century the Lozi have suffered many losses. Their lands, their tradition and even their identity have been whittled away.

Urban southern Africa

alf the Republic of South Africa's 22 million people live in cities and towns. Of the four million white South Africans, all but half a million are urban; almost all the Indians live in the towns, and so do three-quarters of the Cape Coloreds. Even the largest of the four official population groups, the black people (or Bantu), number five million in the urban areas, twice as many as in 1950.

South Africa's rapid industrialization, made possible by its mineral riches, began in the 1930s and gained impetus during World War II. It has transformed the country into an advanced technological and industrial state among the world's first 15 trading nations. All its industrial activity takes place in about four or five distinct areas centered on the main towns. This concentration has thrown peoples of very different culture and race into close proximity. The social and political consequences have been enormous.

It has created havoc among traditional ways of life. It has sucked people from rural South Africa to the cities, first the white countryfolk, the Afrikaners, descendants of the pastoral Boers, and then the Bantu tribesmen from their ancient homelands. The English-speaking whites, much fewer than the Afrikaners, were less affected since most towns had in the first place sprung up around their own pioneering commercial and mining activities.

In modern South Africa the industrial revolution which created the great urban complexes most affected two groups: the white Afrikaners and the black Africans, and they now play the leading roles in the unfolding drama of southern Africa – the Afrikaners because they have political power over the industrial giant, the Africans because they provide five million of the seven million labor force that keeps the giant in motion. The English-speakers, as busy as ever in their chosen sphere of business, watch the others from the political sidelines and observe that two generations of city life have created a new kind of Afrikaner and a new kind of African.

Other territories of southern Africa, notably Rhodesia, mirror the pattern of South Africa's industrialization and urbanization. The main towns of Rhodesia, both in appearance and in their multi-racial populations, have similarities with the towns of the Republic. But in Rhodesia everything is on a much smaller scale; you could, after all, accommodate every white Rhodesian in a single South African city; while the urban blacks of the Republic outnumber all the black Rhodesians put together. The other territories of southern Africa all have distinctive characteristics of their own. Rhodesia is in many ways the colonial Englishman's South Africa. There are two basic reasons for this. First, Rhodesia is fundamentally English in atmosphere, despite the large influx of Spaniards, Portuguese and Italians since the Unilateral Declaration of Independence in 1965, and despite the fact that Africans outnumber Europeans by 25 to one, Rhodesia was, among other things, Cecil

White men first settled in
Rhodesia in the 1890s. Since
the 1920s they have been
governing their new country.
Most have come from Britain.

The 'Soweto' townships have a population of 600,000 Bantu who work in Johannesburg and the mines. Many have homes in the all-African 'Bantustans'.

(Bottom) Flat-topped Table Mountain rises from the shores of Table Bay to tower over Cape Town, where the first Dutch came to settle in 1652.

Rhodes' answer to the Dutchness of South Africa.

The chief difference between the Rhodesian capital of Salisbury and the cosy – detractors would say smug – serenity of Surrey and the rest of suburban England is the abundant supply in Rhodesia of sun and servants, who are of course black. Croquet, cricket and afternoon tea is an attainable ideal. White Rhodesian supporters of the government that declared UDI still love England as well as hating it. Angry complaints that even the British Conservative Party has gone communist may well be followed by bleak sentimentality and songs of the 1950s from way back 'home'.

White Rhodesians in the cities, like their South African counterparts, tend to be affluent – Salisbury has the highest rate of swimming-pools per head in the world. But the second reason why Englishmen often prefer Rhodesia to South Africa is that life is slower, there is far less of the cut and thrust that you witness on the faces and in the movements of South African townspeople. In Salisbury there is always time for one more beer. Here is surely the last outpost of the colonial mentality – replete with knee-flapping khaki shorts, long woolen stockings and Baden-Powell hats. And Rhodesia is cleaner than South Africa, you often hear white Rhodesians say.

Certainly there are many dynamic people in Rhodesia, but there is nevertheless an air of old-fashioned leisure. Perhaps the mood reaches down to the ill-paid African house-servants who earn about $40 a month. Though as

White suburban Johannesburg – with its smart villas and swimming pools – reflects the wealth of the Rand, South Africa's fabulous gold field.

(Over page) Potions for all ills are available in the African medicine shops. Leopard fur is valued for vigor, powdered rhinoceros horn for potency.

33

yet there is no far-reaching policy of separate development (apartheid), Africans live apart from Europeans, the townspeople in shanty dwellings. But they suffer less degradation than their South African counterparts – they have more security, they live in smaller groups, there is less crime, life is more casual.

The Portuguese cities – and they are officially parts of Portugal, just as Kent is part of England and Kentucky part of the USA – have their own strong flavor reminiscent of the cities of South America. Streets in cities like Lourenço Marques in Mozambique or Luanda in Angola are straight and long, laid out like the grandiose *avenidas* of Lisbon and Madrid. There are street cafés in contrast to the closed-in eating houses of South Africa. There is good wine and – in Mozambique's cities – delicious prawns.

There is fierce fighting between Portuguese and African nationalist forces in the hinterland, but the cities are placid. Intermarriage is encouraged and racial intermingling is happy. African nationalists say the Europeans are merely turning the Africans into puppet white men while despising black culture. Nevertheless street scenes are relaxed in contrast to those in South Africa, and black girls say laughingly 'our national color is coffee'.

The aura of Germany ever pervades Windhoek, the capital of South-west Africa (or Namibia). The German-speaking populace still wield influence. You can see square three-storeyed wooden houses with shutters – you could be on the edge of Bavarian Munich. At evening in the *bierhaus* men thump their thighs at rollicking good yarns and exclaim *Jawohl!* In daytime efficiency and decorum sets the German tone.

The capitals of Lesotho, Botswana and Swaziland are small cities into which white South Africans throw themselves with abandon once released from the puritanism and racial divisions of their homeland. Each of these newly independent states' capitals has its own character, but Mbabane in Swaziland, set in the basin below huge mountains of a striking vivid green, takes the prize for beauty. But the towns of these black-governed countries are few and small.

Different and varied they may be, but none of the cities of southern Africa, whether Portuguese, English, German or African in mood or appearance, can completely escape the all-powerful influence of the biggest city in the region; Johannesburg.

This is the legendary City of Gold. Johannesburg is known as 'Goli' to the thousands of black miners from many parts of southern and central Africa who have worked in the alleys and passageways that go down 6,000 feet below the streets which themselves are 5,000 feet above the sea. Old men, both white and black, still talk of the early days when, after the fabulous Witwatersrand gold reef was discovered in 1886, prospectors set up a mining center with tents in rectangular lines like a Roman camp. The lines are there still – the criss-crossing streets

White South Africa's Springbok rugby team has a wildly enthusiastic following. With politics rather fraught, sport has a near-obsessive appeal.

(Bottom) The legislative capital of South Africa, Cape Town is the oldest town, enjoys a Mediterranean climate, and is a major international port.

In Bulawayo, Rhodesia, a Matabele *ayah* (native nanny) minds the baby while her mistress does the shopping in the local center.

of central Johannesburg, but the tents have given way to skyscrapers. The city of a million and a half inhabitants lies astride the gold reef that runs for 120 miles in the shape of a horse-shoe, from Evander in the east to Klerksdorp in the west.

To the north lies Pretoria, the old Boer seat of President Kruger and today the administrative capital of the country. But even Pretoria seems more and more part of the new industrial world that has spread outwards from Johannesburg, along through the reef mining towns and southward to the banks of the Vaal River at Vereeninging. Johannesburg is the industrial heart of the country, though factories now make twice as big a contribution to the national wealth as the mines. In Johannesburg and this surrounding southern Transvaal you can see what all this has meant in human terms: the symbols of wealth as well as the degradation that come in the wake of industrialization.

For a newcomer to Johannesburg first impressions are deceptive. The only South African city with the atmosphere of a great metropolis, 'down-town' Johannesburg with its skyscrapers, fly-over roads going north and south, east and west, its busy shopping centers, office blocks and traffic jams, might be a modern American city. There is a thrusting, dynamic quality in the way the people in the streets, both white and black, go about their business. They look sophisticated 20th century people far removed from the traditional ox-wagon culture of the old Transvaal Boers or the beads and calabash world of the Bantu tribes. Johannesburg at work is a crucible, in which the old inherited cultures mix uneasily, sometimes explosively, with the new values and needs of modern South Africa.

In South Africa this is never more true than in the sphere of race relations for, if during the working day black and white are seen together in the streets, in the shops, in the offices and factories, at the end of it they return to their separate worlds. By six o'clock in the evening central Johannesburg is as quiet and deserted as the financial City of London on a Sunday.

People work there; they do not live there. Urban South Africans are really suburban people. And each of the four racial groups has by law its own area of suburbia to live in. To drive through the affluent northern suburbs of Johannesburg, which stretch a dozen miles or more towards Pretoria, is to be aware of the great wealth created by the City of Gold, for the symbols of wealth are everywhere at hand: beautiful homes in park-like gardens 37

Urban southern Africa

Unlike South Africa, Rhodesia has no official *apartheid* (policy of separation). Yet, except in the university, social mixing is rare.

(Bottom) Daughters of white Rhodesians go to schools modeled on middle class English ones, with an emphasis on swimming, tennis and manners.

(Bottom) The Christian churches — many of them splinter groups — play a big role in giving South African blacks the continent's highest literacy rate.

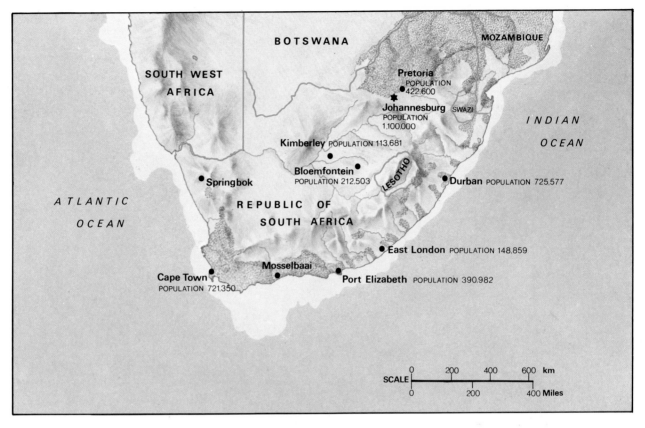

with swimming pools and tennis courts, all forever enveloped in the purple haze of jacaranda trees. And if the gardens are more lavish, more exotic than one might find in England, the names of many of these suburbs, Sandhurst, Hurlingham, Sandringham, as well as some of its churches – St. Martin's-in-the-Veldt, for instance – are a nostalgic reminder of where their owners had their ancestry and acquired their love of gardens. Johannesburg remains a predominantly English city and the life of the northern suburbs with its gardens and country clubs, the golf, the bowls, the polo, and its many cultural pursuits, is reminiscent of a leisured way of life that largely disappeared from Britain with World War I.

South Africa, however, is a country which defies facile generalization and if there is much in the manner of living of Johannesburg which a distinguished French visitor once called *très brittanique,* he would need to be reminded that many English-speaking South Africans are not of British origin. South Africa has a Jewish population of 120,000, most of them in the Transvaal and mainly in Johannesburg, a great many of whom trace their origins to continental Europe, to the Baltic States, to Germany and central Europe. Their contribution to the making of urban South Africa has been enormous. They have not only used business and professional skills to the full, but their special artistic talents have often helped to civilize an often over-materialistic climate.

They have helped build the basis for the flourishing cultural life of cities like Johannesburg.

Hillbrow, the Latin Quarter or Chelsea of Johannesburg, is the cultural center of the urban melting pot. Situated on a high ridge a mile from central Johannesburg, it accentuates its position and character by thrusting its multitude of skyscraper flat-dwellings, like a clutch of insulting fingers, into a jagged skyline. This is cosmopolitan South Africa where many different cultural influences mingle colorfully: there are Jewish art galleries, Greek restaurants, Portuguese vegetable shops, German beerhalls, nightclubs and a night bank, and in the streets by day the young, both white and black, wear the pop uniform of the young everywhere.

Hillbrow has its paler counterparts in other South African cities; it is looked on with disfavor by the conventional English-speakers of the northern suburbs and with alarm by rural Afrikaners fearful for the morals of their sons and daughters, but Hillbrow is a significant initiator in constantly changing Southern African urban society. It is understandable that so many Johannesburgers enjoy weekends in the racially free-for-all, smart hotels and casinos of the independent black-governed states of Swaziland and Lesotho which lie within driving distance from Johannesburg. These could be part of Hillbrow, but Hillbrow being in the Republic of South Africa must submit to the puritan narrowmindedness 39

Urban southern Africa

Inhabitants of black townships
live with the knowledge that
if they lose their jobs they
may be hustled back to the
tribal, all-African homelands.

During the working day blacks and whites mingle in the streets of 'Goli' but in the evening they return to their separate worlds.

which still pervades much of South African legislation as do the attitudes of the 'Wee Free' strict Presbyterian sect which survive in the north of Scotland.

Sunday observance remains a powerful feature, forbidding Sunday cinemas, newspapers, official sport and even light music in the airplanes of the national airline. South Africans do read newspapers on Sunday but they are published late on Saturday. What is particularly noticeable is the success of the Afrikaans Sunday Press of the Transvaal representing urban Afrikaners who want to make South African social attitudes harmonize a little better with the modern physical façade of their cities. At last they have managed to get television. It is difficult to imagine a modern urban environment without it – but South Africa provides the exception. Controversy has raged for many years and rural Afrikaners claimed television was immoral. But according to an official announcement, it is to be introduced during the mid-1970s. Little by little, it seems, the urban Afrikaner, now 70 per cent of Afrikanerdom, is growing in influence.

In South African cities there is no legislation to compel the English-speakers and the Afrikaans-speaking whites to live separately, but on the whole they tend to do so quite voluntarily. In Johannesburg the affluent English-speakers live in Houghton or Hurlingham, while affluent Afrikaners prefer Emmarentia or Linden. They may all be bankers or mining directors or the heads of insurance companies and in their business day English and Afrikaner might meet in the course of conducting their affairs, but there are separate Afrikaner banks and English banks, Afrikaner mining houses and English mining houses. The Afrikaner since World War II has penetrated the traditional English field of commerce and industry, but he has gone along a separate road, creating his own separate commercial and financial institutions.

Many of the Afrikaner business leaders, the tycoons of South African towns today, come from families which in the 1940s were modest countryfolk on their farms. The migration of the rural Afrikaners was a result of the world-wide depression of the early 1930s.

This was the era of the poor whites, when the government was forced to bring in all kinds of schemes to provide work. South Africa has always had a white working class – the railway gangers, postmen, the lorry drivers and bus conductors. In the 1930s the rural Afrikaner, unable to make a living on the land, often came into the towns at this level. Business activity in the towns began to expand and during World War II, when South Africa was cut off from Europe and compelled to manufacture for itself, this expansion galloped away. Urban Afrikaners became established and their children, growing up in a new environment, were taught the values of sticking together socially and working together as urban Afrikaners. Afrikaners and English-speakers in the cities today have very much the same occupations, but they have different languages, churches, schools,

41

Riot control has for long been a specialized art in Africa. In relatively peaceful Rhodesia, dogs are used more for intimidation than their bite.

Urban southern Africa

clubs, and parallel social institutions, such as the Voortrekkers, equivalent of the English community's Boy Scouts. Fusion of the cultural groups is unlikely.

The different customs of Afrikaners and English-speakers may be simply illustrated in a dozen ways. In church, for instance, Afrikaner men stand to pray while the women remain seated; Afrikaners tend to drink tea at 11 o'clock in the morning which is often coffee time for the English, while the traditional English afternoon tea is coffee time for the Afrikaner. In recent years, however, tea distributors have reported a growing tendency among urban Afrikaners to turn to tea at any time. Another example of a change in the urban Afrikaner is his attitude to cricket. This was always regarded as an English game and Afrikaners would not play it; in the 1920s and 1930s when the Springboks were playing England Afrikaners would ask: 'Who's winning, our English or theirs?' Nowadays Afrikaners not only play cricket but follow the country's cricketing fortunes with the same passion they have always shown for the game of rugby football, at which they have long excelled.

The inevitable pressures of a shrinking world, arising out of rapid communication – the influence of films,

books, newspapers and the uniformity of what one buys in shops to eat or wear, above all pop culture among the young – are bringing the two urban communities closer together. Even more important for the future, they are becoming more curious about the black urban community.

Whereas it was the depression of the early 1930s which brought the Afrikaners to the towns, it was the booming economy of the war years, when so many white South Africans, English and Afrikaner, were away at the war fronts in the armed forces, which brought the Bantu in their thousands into the cities. They came not only to Johannesburg and Kimberley, but to the main ports – Cape Town, Durban, Port Elizabeth and East London. They came with their families and in great hopes, but these were short-lived: although there were jobs, the cities had neither the housing nor other amenities to receive them. The story of these years is the story of a rural, simple people trying, in the most appalling conditions of the shantytowns they created, to adjust to an urban environment totally strange to people relying on the security of the tribe. In time order took over from chaos and the shantytowns were replaced by a vast

A Cape Malay marriage in Cape Town: the rites are traditional Muslim, but the language is Afrikaans and the clothes mainly western.

(Bottom) Peasant Portuguese have gone to live in Angola in their thousands, homesteading among local Africans in a racially relaxed, paternal role.

sprawling monotony of tiny bungalows, clustered in the townships, a feature of all South African cities.

To fly over Johannesburg today is to see that it is not one but two cities, for the collection of 26 townships, known collectively as Soweto, form a large rival city in the south-west. Some 600,000 Bantu live in Soweto, and here, by suburban train and bus, all those Africans on the streets of Johannesburg by day disappear at night. As with white Johannesburg, Soweto has its comparatively affluent areas and its poor areas, but the poor areas vastly outnumber the rich. It has shopping centers, churches, sports stadiums and swimming pools, but the fact of having to build for so many so quickly has created a nightmare of architecture and planning.

The population of Soweto is as big as Botswana's and bigger than Swaziland's. It is predominantly Sotho and Nguni, but there are also members of the Venda, Tsonga and Ndebele peoples. However, after more than a quarter of a century of urbanization, the township African has emerged from places like Soweto and its smaller equivalents in other cities as a distinct phenomenon, and he now feels very little tribal pull. In the

This woman's face, whitened with ash as a pagan sign of sanctity, represents a soul yet unconverted for this priest in Mozambique city.

43

Urban southern Africa

same way that Afrikaans writers such as Jochem van Bruggen with his immortal novel *Ampie* described the plight of the poor white, African writers such as Ezekiel Mphalele have written of the difficult adaptation of the Bantu to the life of the towns, a life made infinitely complicated and precarious by the involved rules and regulations governing his existence in towns, officially white, since they are not in the Bantu homelands.

The overriding factor in the lives of the five million urban Africans is their sense of insecurity, since they are officially regarded as being only temporarily in the towns. There is the fear of losing a job and with it the right to stay on as an urban dweller. And every Bantu in what is officially a white homeland must hold various passes, the product perhaps of influx control. Failures to produce the pass – perhaps because it has been lost or left in the house may land a good man or woman in prison. Despite, or perhaps because of, their difficulties and adversities, much that is exciting, new and cultural has emerged from the urban Africans. There is a new, racy, Damon Runyon type of English that runs through African journalism and writing; there is the distinctive township music which is broadcast regularly by Radio Bantu, whose services go out in seven languages to several million listeners. As in the white suburbs, a small growing bourgeoisie has emerged in the black townships. Class and status symbols, encouraged by advertising, are everywhere. The motor car – and 100,000 Africans own one – is an important status symbol.

One of the most remarkable aspects of urban African life is the new position that women have won for themselves. The Zulu *isidwaba,* the leather kilt worn by married women in tribal society, has suffered the same fate as the apron and bra; it has been cast away in the manner of other women's liberation movements. Wigs, skinlightening lotions and false eye-lashes have become part of the African woman's paraphernalia in her new urban environment where she fills a variety of skilled and professional occupations. Women, too, play an important part in the religious life of the townships.

Symbolic of the confusion wrought in the lives of African tribesmen by the advent of white men and their religion is the profusion of Bantu separatist churches, about 2,000 of them. Many have grown up round individual Bantu prophets such as Isaiah Shembe in Natal and they practise a curious mixture of Christian and pagan rites. In most South African towns at the week-ends members of these sects, dressed in their particular uniforms and singing their religious songs parade through the streets.

A feature of the life in and around Cape Town, South Africa's original urban area, is the distinctive Cape Colored people. There are two million of them and 90 per cent live at the Cape, where they are particularly active in the fishing industry. They are descendants of unions between early settlers and indigenous Hottentots

The 2 million Cape Coloreds are descendants of early settlers and Hottentots or imported slaves. Many today live by fishing.

or imported slaves. They belong to the western European cultural heritage, and although they have a folk tradition of their own, particularly in music and stories, they are culturally very close to the Afrikaners, mostly sharing their language and religion. Many liberal Afrikaners, in fact, regard the Cape Coloreds as 'Brown Afrikaners' and acknowledge the contribution that the Coloreds, particularly their poets, have made to Afrikaans literature.

Officially part of the Coloreds group but maintaining a separate identity because of their Muslim religion are the 60,000 Cape Malays, who are easy to distinguish in the streets of Cape Town. The men wear a red fez, while the women go veiled. Their religious books are written in Afrikaans but with Arabic characters. Many are skilled tradesmen and live in Cape Town's Malay Quarter, well-known for its restored 18th century houses.

Whereas the Coloreds are associated with the Cape, the Indians are almost exclusively residents of Natal to whose sugar plantations their ancestors came from India as indentured labor in the 19th century. The Indian community of Durban has become highly prosperous and industrious, running its own businesses, its own bank, hotels and cinemas and at the Orient Club their élite gather in surroundings which parallel those of the whites' Durban Club or the Jewish Club. Neither Hindus nor Muslims have lost their cultural heritage of religious festivals, dances and music after a century of close proximity to the essentially English population of Natal. The relations of the Indians with the whites are usually friendly, though each group is independent of the other: where each one lives and works has been determined by the racial zoning laws. A town such as Verulum, for instance, north of Durban, is now a largely Indian town with an Indian mayor.

But in white-ruled urban southern Africa, particularly in South Africa itself, there is more and more mutual curiosity and stronger desire for contact between the different population groups, mainly in professional and business circles, despite the laws or customs of apartheid. At the higher level of city life a community of interests is breaking down racial and cultural differences. Nevertheless the danger of friction caused by the close proximity of culturally and racially different peoples is always present. Sometimes, too, the violence of antique Africa erupts disconcertingly in a modern setting, as for instance when two rival Zulu factions, drawn up in ancient battle order, fought a murderous battle in the sophisticated streets of Johannesburg.

45

Miners of southern Africa

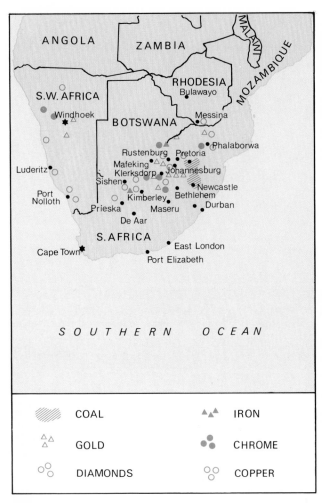

COAL

GOLD

DIAMONDS

IRON

CHROME

COPPER

Every morning at dawn groups of African gold miners on the daytime shift are brought from the African townships on the edge of Johannesburg by bus to the mines. They crowd into wire cage lifts and are lowered many feet into the mine. Like all mines, it is hot – the temperature is often more than 100° fahrenheit – and, at the face, dusty and noisy from the operation of the power drills. The foremen and senior mechanics are mostly white men. It is tough work for many; yet the mines are among the best equipped in the world. At the exit to the mines, the men are thoroughly searched.

Southern Africa is an Aladdin's cave of mineral wealth: the diamonds of Kimberley and the gold of Johannesburg are famous throughout the world. In Angola there are diamonds and iron, in South-west Africa there are diamonds, copper, lead and zinc, and many other minerals. Botswana has diamonds. Swaziland is rich in iron. Rhodesia is rich in asbestos, coal, copper and chrome. Zambia is a leading copper producer.

By far the richest country in minerals is South Africa itself. It is the world's largest producer of diamonds by value. Since 1953 it has been the world's biggest producer

47

The gold mining industry
provides a livelihood for
about half of the South
African population; the income
is steady but the work is hard.

of platinum. And it is among the world's most important producers of uranium. Most important of all, although South Africa covers only 0.8 per cent of the world's surface, and houses only 0.5 per cent of the world's people, it produces three quarters of the free world's gold. South Africa is also a leading producer of iron ore, chromite and coal, and also on a smaller scale mines copper, silver, nickel, magnesium, tungsten, lead, mercury and many other minerals. In 1970 more than 656,000 men, mostly black Africans, were working at any one time in these various mines. Some 200,000 Africans come into South Africa every year on temporary passes from neighboring African-ruled countries (some as distant as Kenya and Tanzania) to work in the mines, and another fifteen or twenty thousand smuggle themselves in, drawn by the relatively high earnings and the bright lights.

Except for the state-controlled diamond mining at Alexandra Bay, the South African mining industry is run by public companies, though through taxation and mining leases the state has become the largest shareholder of the gold-mining industry. The state gets about 46 per cent of the profits, while private shareholders get about 39 per cent. The government runs a famous metallurgical laboratory in Johannesburg, which has developed important new processes for extracting uranium, andalusite, chromite and other minerals. It also conducts research into mineral processing for atomic power.

South Africa's vast coal fields have not yet been fully opened up, but there are known deposits of 75,000 tons lying deep under the soil. Copper and gold on the other hand were known and smelted centuries before the arrival of Europeans, but further north in what is now Zambia, Rhodesia and eastern and north Transvaal, by a people subsequently dislodged by migrations of warlike peoples like the Matabele. Copper was the first valuable metal won in large quantities after the European occupation of South Africa. The Namaqualand Field, for example, was discovered in 1685. As early as 1797 an Englishman had brought a 57 carat diamond from an African for a guinea. Diamond mining in South Africa began in earnest in 1869 when a diamond rush followed the discovery of the *Star of Africa* diamond. The face of South Africa was to be unalterably changed by a chance event in 1886 when George Walker stumbled on an outcrop of gold-bearing reef on the 'Ridge of White Waters'. From all over the world prospectors rushed to the Witwatersrand, and the shanty town of Johannesburg mushroomed into the vast city that it is today. The central Witwatersrand produced half the Republic's gold until the nearby Klerksdorp mine took precedence after World War II. Since then the Orange Free State and the East Transvaal Highveldt have been developed, and the techniques of mining have improved at revolutionary speeds. Men are now mining at more than two miles below the surface at East Rand Proprietary Mines, and

will soon be working even further down. Conditions in the mines have improved too. Fatal accidents have been sharply reduced to 0.123 per cent a year, and the death rate from mining diseases like tuberculosis and silicosis is almost equally low. Of the 656,000 men who work underground, 80 per cent are black Africans, or Bantu – as the white South Africans call them. Until recently there was little training for the work. Now Bantu laborers have to take aptitude tests. Some are trained as supervisors and have superior status and living quarters. All the men are trained above ground in replicas of underground conditions by methods that involve the simplest of visual aids to overcome language barriers and cultural differences between the various tribesmen.

It is a labor force made up of men whose previous lives have been tribal, traditional and built around status, kinship and personal relations. The relationship of these men to their work is totally different from that of the average European or American. For the black worker a move to the mines, even for a short time, is more than a change of occupation. It is a change in the whole pattern of his life. Many of the men who come to the mines for the first time have never traveled in any kind of modern vehicle. Many have never seen a train, a bus, a car. Some have never learned to use spades or hammers, and very few have ever had boots or shoes on their feet. Even the most routine aspects of their new activities will be entirely new experiences: wearing western clothes and safety helmets, sitting in classrooms or dining rooms, even walking on concrete. Since the recruits speak many different languages, many of which are unrelated, they are instructed in a common language full of special mining terms called *fanakalo,* which is spoken by Africans, and white men alike. This in itself could be traumatic. The medical care that the black Africans receive free from the state is very different from, or even contradictory to, bush medicine. They eat some European food, but also a maize poridge, *lambulazi,* and a maize-based beer called *mahewu.*

The mine authorities claim that the miner's standard of living is better than it could ever be in his tribal village. They have a point. The alternative is subsistence farming at home. White control and settlement in southern Africa, indeed the intrusion of western ideas and practices throughout Africa, have anyway reduced the traditional activities of African men: game has become scarce and colonial or settler rule long since virtually eliminated tribal warfare. Among most tribes women are the cultivators and agricultural workers; men are invariably underemployed, according to western notions. Theoretically a job in the mines can offer a man some hope of bettering his traditional tribal life without actually changing it. When a miner comes home wages saved in the mines can buy his cattle, asserting his status as a tribesman.

It is not difficult for mining companies to recruit young

Diamonds were first discovered at Kimberley in 1869, and the African labor force had to be encouraged to migrate there on a temporary basis.

The end-product glitters indeed — but the gold ore is of low grade and it is seldom found at less than 4,000 feet below the surface.

White mining unions ensure certain jobs are 'reserved' for their own kind. Yet the two races work well together, as here, in the smelting process.

49

men from a wide area, bind them by contract for a specific period, and house them for their period of employment in compounds, which is cheaper than housing whole families. In the compounds the men are easy to supervise. Under the watchful eye of the foreman, drunkenness, absenteeism and theft – a particular danger in the diamond industry – can be restrained.

Broadly speaking there is a threefold pattern in this movement to the mines from their tribal subsistence economies. Some of the men who move have every intention of eventually returning to their families. Their aim is to earn enough money in the mines to support themselves, and send home, or bring home, enough of a surplus to improve their families' status and standard of living. In these cases family and village life, although disrupted by the father's absence, continues on much the same pattern. The children grow up in their traditional environment and have little contact with modern development. There are other men who sign on for the mines who take their families to live with them in the mining areas. This has the virtue of keeping families together, but subjects them to traumatic changes in environment and life-style, to a radical disorientation in the tightly packed urban surroundings, with all this power manifestly in white hands. These families tend to get the worst of both worlds. They lose the psychological support of

their own ancient, stable, peasant backgrounds, without earning enough to enjoy much of the material comforts of white urban civilization. Yet other miners have simply rejected traditional life – and perhaps very often family responsibilities as well – and go off to earn money which they keep for themselves. They tend not to come home when their contract expires. The wages for which all the young men interrupt or abandon their tribal life are, by West European or American standards, pitifully small – about the same as those in China. Since 1969 the minimum wage has been 10.42 rand, about $15, a month.

Mining recruitment, although well organized, is very different from the formal system of indentured labor that brought Indians to South Africa or Chinese to Malaya. Recruitment is energetic and persuasive and extends far beyond the areas immediately around the mines in question: the Witwatersrand Native Labor Association (Wenela) goes as far afield as Malawi and Mozambique in search of labor, and maintains its own aircraft to bring recruits to the mines and take them home when their contracts expire.

This recruitment system is a matter of free choice: there is no compulsion, and the same areas go on producing labor, largely through the recommendation of those who have done a spell in the mines. Many keep going back. Yet when a migrant worker finds himself

Deprived of women and family life, miners find a welcome emotional outlet in tribal dances, performed in traditional feathered style.

When gold was discovered in the 19th century, the government allotted prospectors square plots from which they could start digging down.

The Finsch mine and recovery plant was opened in 1967. It was the first diamond pipe mine to be opened in South Africa since 1903.

lodged within a mining company's compound, he finds that he enjoys only an ambiguous sort of freedom, comparable to that of an enlisted man in the armed services. He is not, strictly, a prisoner. On the other hand, his work and also his residence are governed by a contract, breach of which is a criminal offense and not merely (as in English or American law) a civil offense. His right to go into the city and take his ease, during his off-duty hours, is limited and conditional upon good behavior.

Even his wages will not be paid to him freely: many companies pay wages in a lump sum at the end of a contract, to avoid wild spending and trouble during the term of the contract. And many companies pay wages only on a miner's arrival home. They feel that he should buy a cow or a wife, something useful, rather than spend it all at once in the excitement at release from a year or more of regimentation.

The compounds where the miners live are not homely. The buildings are solid, the streets and pathways are well-paved. There are communal kitchens serving food that is very likely more nutritious than village food. There are laundries and lavatories. And food and medical services are provided. Many miners are physically fitter in the compounds than they would be back in their home villages. It is also true that the compounds provide entertainment – especially dancing. Tribal dances are not only fun to watch – they are the subject of enthusiastic competition between miners from many different places and different tribes. Dances are staged regularly, often weekly, and with a wide variety of costumes, feathers and weapons and a thunderously rich texture of often erotic movement they are an enthralling spectacle. The mining companies encourage entertainment of this sort. And there are swimming pools and stadiums.

Yet the gridded compounds, each identical, suggest army barracks, rather than hostels for civilian workmen. There is little privacy, life is routine, and lacks the warmth of real community life. There is always a certain amount of homosexuality; the miners have few alternative sexual outlets. And with so many men crowded together aggression and friction are unavoidable. The realities of home and relations in the country are far away: migration of labor must be expected to have bad effects within both family and job.

The system under which miners live and work disturbs many, both inside South Africa and beyond although the gold mining industry especially has earned a good name for labor relations. Government regulations in South Africa limit the benefits of mining for the miners. To implement the apartheid policy by limiting the growth of African communities in white areas, they restrict the number of family houses that can be built for African mineworkers. The system of migrant and temporary labor living in compounds is thus perpetuated; and black Africans continue to be uprooted partly at the expense of the security of traditional life.

51

Xhosa, Pondo, Tembu, Swazi
South Africa

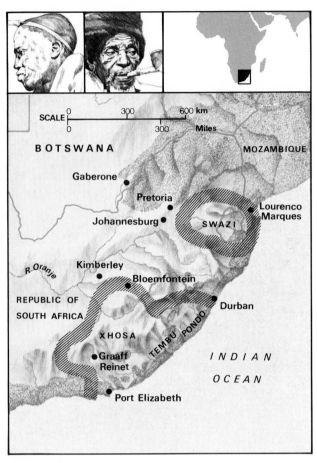

To give your own interpretation of the society you were born and brought up in is risky. Impressions and emphases are so different for different readers. If the readers are fellow-members of your society they tend to seek only praise. If they are outsiders to it they suspect any praise as chauvinism. If they are specialist observers such as anthropologists or sociologists, they will feel that in some passages you exaggerate and that in others you are too skimpy; or that you have omitted this or invented that. My refuge, in writing about the Xhosa society I belong to, is in that wise comment made by the anthropologist B Malinowski: 'The vision of the past in human memory and tribal legend is something which has to be studied. It has a psychological influence active in present-day African society. People are swayed by the *errors* they *feel* and not by the *truth* which they *ignore*'. Anything I write here should indubitably be regarded in the light of what it felt like to belong to this society.

To be a member of the Xhosa people of my generation, born just over 50 years ago in troubled South Africa, was to be very much aware, as one grew up, of being a descendant of the Nguni section of those Bantu-speaking tribes which traveled down the south-eastern plateau to

53

A young Xhosa, recently
circumcised, has his face
and body painted white.
Custom forbids him contact
with women at this time.

Xhosa initiates share a
secluded hut after the
circumcision ceremony. For
three months their food must
be prepared by a man.

the tip of Africa, over a conjectured period of 5,000 years.

Bantu-speakers had no writing and handed down their histories in an oral tradition. As the centuries pass historical facts become distant in time. They become remote, then legendary. There is the legendary Togu, the distant figure of the forefather – *ingotya*. When telling the story of Xhosa descent, old men traced the royal line back as far as possible and on reaching his resounding name, they paused for breath, unable to delve further into the mists of time; and exclaimed triumphantly 'There then is the forefather – *ingotya*!' From Togu the Nguni family tree spreads out as the patrilinear forbears emerge.

But the remotest legendary ancestral ruler from whom the Xhosa are conscious of being descended is Mnguni. Xhosa legend in relation to the advent of man on earth may be compared with that of Adam in the garden of Eden. 'The Great One Up Above – Unkulunkulu' plucked a reed from the river-bed, split it and Mnguni appeared. Having appeared, he begat, as man does. As no record has been handed down of the existence of a lady, the acceptable inference is that the founder of the Mnguni peoples must have been a hermaphrodite. No matter. According to Xhosa belief, all Nguni peoples are his issue. Centuries passed. It is because Mnguni is so distant that his descendants the Xhosa, and the Tembu, Bomvana, Pondo, Zulu and others – call themselves Nguni only

generically. Each branch of his descendants has its own ancestor of whom they know as well as Mnguni, a benevolent ectoplasm, in the background. These peoples use as their present-day names the names of their kings of living tribal memory. A Xhosa will say he is 'of-Ndamase' or 'of-Ngqika'; a Pondo will say he is 'of-Ndamase' or 'of-Faku', or 'of-Mditshwa' and so on.

Tracing royal lineages is complicated by the fact that a sovereign had two heirs, two eldest sons. There was the prince of the Great House, who succeeded the king and inherited all his property, and the prince of the Right Hand House, who was required, when his brother became king, to move away out of the new monarch's sight. The shadows of kings must not collide. The prince of the Great House claimed the obedience and respect of all his brothers and half-brothers however much older than himself. Thus, a sovereign's family was positively stoloniferous – like the branches of a tree. The brothers and their sons were subordinate to the heir and to his sons forever.

In the eastern Cape, the Jingqhi Xhosas are descendants of the Right Hand. By the time Gcaleka had reached the Kei River and inherited the sovereignty, his Right Hand brother heir, Ngqika had to move away, across the river and found a new dynasty.

It seems that when European adventurers first knew of

Xhosa huts are made of woven wattles plastered with mud. Some Xhosa tightly shut the door and tiny window at night to keep out witches.

the presence of black people in the eastern Cape Province of South Africa, the Xhosa tribe had reached down into what is now Lesotho. Individuals resembling them (black, chocolate brown, medium height) were spotted in this area by long-sighted Portuguese sailors during the 16th century, according to records these mariners kept, and which may be seen in Lisbon's archives.

Those black natives the Portuguese saw, presumably in the distance for the Nguni were not sea-farers, were members of the Ama-Jingqhi clan of the Xhosa. Xhosa people are inordinately proud of being the southernmost of all Africans, and the proudest are the Jingqhi for having achieved this feat of migration.

Of course, people did not know the term 'Africa'. They knew from legends only that they had traveled south, conquering and partially absorbing other peoples on the way, especially the Hottentots. It was the mission-aries – *abefundisi* – who first taught about the vast continent the Creator made when creating land, sea and sky; man and beast; sun, moon and stars. Unaware of being continentals they knew the territories which, as semi-nomadic pastoralists, they had temporarily settled in their search for grazing lands. They named such territories after the ancestral kings who led them. For instance, the Cape Colony, as it was, was known as Emaxhoseni, history having taught that their king,

Xhosa, led and settled them there. The same applied to other Nguni tribes. Swaziland was Kwelamangwane, the king Ngwane having led his followers there. Southern Portuguese East Africa was Kwelaba Tshangane, the ruler Sotshangane having done likewise.

The power of black people's kings has long been broken. And as a result of Boer domination their socio-political organization is a shambles. Yet the current generation of Xhosa and their Nguni relations still feel as they were supposed, by custom, to feel when living under their traditional systems. Merely to gaze on the surrounding landscape is to be reminded of their past. Across the great Kei River one recalls that Gcaleka's land (now called the Transkei) was once beautiful, before the overcrowding and before the soil erosion caused by the confinement of erstwhile roving pastoralists to restricted fenced-off areas of South Africa. It is giant country with Brobdingnagian sweeps of mountains, valleys, plains and skies. It must have been a wrench for the Right Hand heir Ngqika to leave it, as required by the age-old Nguni system, and to strike new ground. Yet the Ciskei, or Ngqikasland, as Xhosas call it was also lovely. When Lord Henry Somerset invaded it he described it:

'The country, billowing away from heights to the east of the Great Fish to the Keiskama river, includes several lofty and lovely mountain ranges. The most famous of 55

In many areas of the Transkei fuel is so scarce that women may have to walk many miles to find firewood and carry it back home.

(Bottom) After circumcision Pondo's faces are smeared with an ant heap solution – they must drink some of it to make their hearts audacious.

(Right) With many a young Nguni away at work on contract in the gold or diamond mines, only the young, old and women remain.

these are the Amatola mountains; then there are the arresting runners-up, the Katberg and Winterberg ranges. The lower slopes of the Amatola are furred with extensive forests, mainly of giant yellow-wood trees. The whole region is one of the most beautiful in South Africa: it is a land of wooden glens and fluted valleys waving with red-brown grass and dappled with green and golden thorn-trees. It is a region rich in historical association and scarred with bloodstained landmarks. The crumbling ruins of long-deserted forts lie scattered near the banks of the bright and beautiful Keiskama. Here also many a rough old tombstone covers the heroic dust of some soldier or settler who died to set the bounds of empire wider yet.' Such is the setting of Ama-Jinghi, the Xhosa-of-Ngqika. Gazing around on it, and seeing the other Ngqikas such as the Ama-Ndhlambe, Ama-Ntinde and so on, a Xhosa even today is conscious of the continuity in the way of life of his people.

Every family household is ordered in the same way. A Xhosa is trained from the family hearth that every man is a man, as is the king, as are the king's sons. The royals are different only because of their greater wealth in the form of cattle. Otherwise all people are absolutely alike. The ideas society enjoins them to hold and the beliefs they must embrace are for everybody the same. The overwhelming idea that every Xhosa must hold is that a human being is a person by virtue of being of other people – *umntu ngumntu ngabantu*. Respect for the personality, the humanness within, is the keynote in dealing with others.

As soon as a young Xhosa can talk his family organizes his behavior in order to make him a social animal. He is taught, for example, that he belongs to an age-group which addresses its immediate seniors and juniors in the ceremonious manner 'Brother So-and-So' or 'Sister So-and-So', and never just baldly 'So-and-So'. The household servants, retainers, dependents, hangers-on, people outside the family circle and every Tom, Dick and

Members of the Gcaleka
family of the Xhosa people
perform a tribal dance in
braided grass skirts, and
wearing grass masks.

Harry must be properly addressed.

He must distinguish between paternal relatives and
maternal relatives between their age-groups, and with
special regard to his own parents. For instance he will
call his uncle who is his father's younger brother 'Little
Father'. He will call his mother's older sister 'Big Mother'.
He is taught this because in some circumstances it is
simply good manners to do so, while in others it is
downright rude, offensive, and therefore strictly forbidden, to forget them. An error may rate a smack or
even a thrashing. A Xhosa is taught which cuts of meat
he may eat and which he may not eat. He is taught who
must be served first and who must hold back. He learns
which members of the family may or may not approach
the cattle enclosure. A woman learns which circuit to
tread in passing the cattle enclosure at certain times of
the month. When he reaches puberty a Xhosa is circumcized along with other boys in his age-group into the
elevated state of maturity. Girls are never circumcized.
This is an operation regarded with horror by Nguni.
But a feast is held to celebrate a girl's first menstruation,
to which all, including passers-by are invited to celebrate,
the information now being broadcast that the daughter
of the house has reached marriageable age. All branches
of Nguni-speakers have similar kinship and marriage
customs that include a belief in exogamy. This belief by
which no couple may marry if four generations back
they had one common ancestor, is held especially strongly
by the Xhosa. These days there are people who sometimes flout this tradition when they marry, refusing to
submit to the examination of their personal family trees.
Their union is frowned upon.

When a Xhosa woman marries
she lengthens her skirts,
wears a different style of
beads and she is allowed
to smoke a pipe.

Jackal hunter turned herbalist, Khatso Suthwata, a Xhosa, has an 'empire' and 20 wives. He has become a legend and a millionaire.

At every passage of a Xhosa – and indeed of all Nguni – from one role to the next in the society framework there are observances to be carried out which dramatize and emphasize the individual's progress towards the respected state of old-age. At every stage of life, a person must respect others, thus to be respected by them . . .

I am trying to show why and how Xhosa people today cling to their inherited beliefs and traditions and why despite the tragedy of their society under apartheid they largely succeed in maintaining an inner equilibrium, to say nothing of maintaining their sense of humor.

Take one last example of this Nguni way of looking at life, and of regarding the person's personality. *Umntu ngunatu ngabantu:* a human being is a person by virtue of being of other people. As their bus traverses the landscape where once battles were fought, a busload of ragged working-class Xhosa, who include former royalty and gentlemen, are inspired to talk of the personalities of Right Hand sons, and sometimes of regencies, of which Nguni history shows an extraordinary number because, as the Great Wife – the wife of the nation – was by custom married by the king late in his life, the heir was almost always an infant, whose brother of the Right Hand had to hold power for him until he came of age. These regents having eaten of the flesh pots of power and privilege for so long would often tend to usurp. In the bus the talk is abundant and deafening on the theme that the nature of a Right Hand prince is necessarily one of twisted cunning. The Right Hand is a dangerous plotter and schemer and by nature a tactician, a man of acumen and resilience. The only real difference between him and us, however, they say, is that his personality is more explosive than that of all of us.

Xhosa people know, because they daily feel and see the evidence, that the human being is of shortlived and violent emotional reactions. Violent. Quick to love unreasonably. Quick to hate and quarrel unreasonably. Quick to forgive and forget unreasonably. He is shallow, a creature of sensations only. Terrible, for that way lies anarchy. And people cannot live as people, as human beings in this condition. So society has devised the means by which this basic savagery can be controlled and contained. Respect. Look ahead. Be kind to strangers and beggars – you may be in need yourself one day. Tactics. Patience. Above all treat that wild inner person with respect, for a person is as nothing. He may be saved only by learning to appreciate that a person is a person by virtue of his being *of* persons: a human being. *Umntu.* 59

Zimbabwe
Rhodesia

The unknown builders of Zimbabwe, Rhodesia, erected this solid tower of dressed stone and 32 foot walls, one of Africa's greatest mysteries.

Perhaps it is Africa's greatest mystery. Dominating the wild bush country south-east of Rhodesia's oldest town, Fort Victoria, the massive ruins of Zimbabwe stand as evidence of a remarkable former African culture – the center of the lost empire of Monomotapa, which thrived half a millennium and more ago on the gold taken from the extensive diggings throughout much of what is now eastern Rhodesia, north-western Mozambique, and southern Zambia, and exported to the Arabs along the coast at Sofala and elsewhere, several hundred miles to the east.

There are no comparable ruins throughout the whole of what is now Bantu Africa. Only at four other sites in the same region has evidence been found of local inhabitants cutting and building in stone – at Khami, Dhlo-dhlo and Naletali, and in remnants of terracing at Inyanga.

The ruins of Zimbabwe comprise the formidable Great Enclosure, 350 feet across. The Great Wall itself is 32 feet high at its highest point, and 16 feet thick at its base. Lesser walls inside enclose smaller areas. The main conical tower in the center of the ruins' elliptical perimeter suggests that it was the focal point of fertility rites, of which rain-making may have been the principal content. In the enclosed space have been found phallic and gold objects, and carved soap-stone pillars and ornaments, including a vulture-like stone bird, possibly representing the feared Hungwe, or fish eagle, which recurs frequently in African legend.

Above the temple, built on the precipitous Zimbabwe hill, stand the remains of an acropolis, demonstrating similar stonework. Within its defenses is a complex of walls, enclosures and platforms, all cleverly integrated with the natural granite boulders that form the summit. Within most of the enclosures were dwellings, and in at least one of them there is evidence of gold working.

Excavations at the site, however, have shown little evidence of any advanced civilization. Objects have been found which testify to a link with south Asia, presumably via the east coast port of Sofala; but the rarity of objects suggests the link was tenuous. Persian beads have been found, and a fragment of Ming china. The architecture of Zimbabwe appears to owe nothing to outside influence, and it looks as if it derives from the round grass huts and pole and straw enclosures that might be found in any southern African village. The workers in stone may well have begun by imitating these basic structures with the new material. Once the builders were inspired with the idea of working in stone, the technical difficulties would not have been too great in a country whose hills are frequently composed of exfoliating granite that splits into 'leaves'. Such leaves would require dressing for building. Although the masons became increasingly ambitious, they did not learn to measure accurately nor to keep a regular distance between two parallel walls or to bond one wall into another. Such sculptured stone birds and carved dishes as have survived are made from soap-

stone, which is exceptionally soft and easy to work.

The mining operations showed considerable organization and technical ability. Many hundreds of ancient mine diggings exist, some of them descending to a depth of a hundred feet. Hundreds of millions of dollars worth of gold must have been exported via Sofala to Kilwa and then to the eastern markets. The trade was still flourishing when the Portuguese first arrived on the coast of eastern Africa, in what is now Mozambique, at the end of the 15th century. Yet the Portuguese could never make the system work. By 1512, the Portuguese Royal Agent, whose countrymen had usurped Arab power at points along the coast, was reporting an average annual export of approximately 100 lbs weight of gold, and somewhat larger quantities of ivory and copper (there were some diggings in Katana), some amber, seed pearls, coral and a few slaves.

A few years later the trade had dried up. The Portuguese never reached Zimbabwe. And by the time the white hunter from South Africa, venturing into what was then unexplored territory in 1868, stumbled on the site, none of the local tribesmen, the Mashona, could give an explanation of who built the extraordinary stone structures or how they came to be there.

No other remotely comparable stone ruins exist in Bantu Africa. The local Mashona tribe today build only in wood, wattle and mud.

Some wood which was found supporting a drain at the base of the main wall of the Great Enclosure of Zimbabwe has been carbon-dated at 800 to 1,000 AD, as the time the tree from which it was made ceased to be alive. This suggests that the main walls were begun at that time. Both Arab, and later Portuguese, chroniclers tell of the existence of the empire or kingdom of Monomotapa (*mwana wa tapa* – 'Lord of Subject Peoples'), from the 15th century.

Whoever initiated Zimbabwe, recent research indicates that at the start of the 15th century a group of Bantu clans came to occupy the south and south-west of today's Rhodesia – a people composed of small-scale cultivators and cattle breeders who practised the typical ancestor cult of their forbears in the region of the Great Lakes. These Vakaranga clans were headed by a particular clan with marked skills, the Barozwi. The name Monomotapa, given to the empire thus established, was the title of the king.

Violent convulsions were already wracking this empire in the early 18th century. It was critically threatened, evidently by a revolt of powerful vassals. Small garrisons of Portuguese were by then established in Sena and Tete, up the Zambezi. A document survives, drawn up by the local Portuguese Commander, Diogo Simoes, by which the Emperor Monomotapa ceded all the mines of 'gold, copper, iron, lead and pewter' to the Portuguese king, in exchange for military assistance.

Portuguese encroachment met with resistance. The Sena and Tete garrisons were destroyed; but the Portuguese held on at the coast through the 17th and 18th centuries. Nevertheless, Barozwi rule was in decline when a Swazi horde, set in motion by the train of tribal wars known as the Mfecane, which ravaged central south-eastern Africa from the mid-18th century to the mid-19th century, broke all but the last shadow of its power around 1820. By then the gold industry had long ceased and Zimbabwe had long been abandoned. Legend tells that the invaders flayed alive the Mambo, or Great Chief, of the Barozwi. The successors of the Barozwi in the region of Monomotapa came to be known as Mashona – a loose *congeries* of tribes closely allied to the Vakarango, who still live alongside them. The word Mashona, used today, is probably a term of contempt applied to them by the newly arrived neighbors, the warlike Matabele.

The Barozwi survive – a tribal remnant – to the south of their former habitat. The legends recall the presence but not the construction of Zimbabwe. To this day, members of the Barozwi tribe have a high reputation among the Mashona for skill in magic. At the summit of ancestral Shona belief stands the mythical Chaminuku who first taught the people how to cultivate certain crops, to make beer and to extract iron from certain rocks. According to Shona legend, Chaminuku made his appearance at Zimbabwe, 'speaking from the air'.

61

Afrikaner farmers
South Africa

Dutch East India Company
ships brought out the first
settlers to South Africa in
the late 17th century — hardy,
Calvinist ex-soldiers.

Once upon a time the burghers of Cape Town could hear lions roaring close up to the wild-almond hedge surrounding their settlement, and hyenas ate dead bodies faster than they could be buried in the countryside around.

Those were the days when ancestors of the Afrikaners, (white South Africans whose mother tongue is Afrikaans), had just arrived at the Cape. Today they number over half the white population of South Africa and have the greatest political influence. But the first Afrikaners were servants of the Dutch East India Chartered Company which had set up a post at the Cape as early as 1652 to revictual their ships sailing to and from the spice islands of the Far East.

The company recruited their servants at its head-quarters in Amsterdam. But their recruits were by no means all Dutchmen. The Thirty Years War which had raged across Europe like a fever had just ended and left ex-soldiers from Denmark, Germany, Switzerland and Flanders who were all looking for the kind of adventure-with-security that the Company had to offer.

But the Garrison at the Cape had to eat as well as guard, and, in 1657 the Company felt obliged to release some of its soldiers from their contracts and establish them as farmers. Grain was needed above all. The Governor, Jan van Riebeeck, had been criticized for importing cereals in ships that could otherwise have carried more valuable cargoes. So the first nine free burghers, all married men of German or Dutch descent, were established in the surrounding countryside on farms of roughly thirty acres. They were forbidden to hunt, to barter with the natives or to infringe the Company's monopoly by selling their produce to passing ships. Yet they prospered; and it became clear to the Company that it would pay to turn their refreshment post into a permanent settlement.

The supply of recruits from Holland dwindled as conditions in Europe improved. But in 1658 the Sun-King Louis XIV repealed the Edict of Nantes which allowed freedom of worship to the French Protestant Huguenots and within months 50,000 of these Huguenot families had braved death or imprisonment to escape across the border and seek refuge in England, Holland, Denmark and other anti-Catholic strongholds. They left their land behind them but took their skills and beliefs, and in no country did they feel so much at home as in Holland where their own fervently austere creed – Calvinism – had become the state religion.

They found in Holland a people who had fought for their faith against that great Catholic, Philip II of Spain, and when the Dutch East India Company offered free passage to a land south of the equator where there were no Catholics but only Dutch Protestants ready to engage with them in a common adventure, the more enterprising Huguenots jumped at the chance.

Seven shiploads of them landed at the Cape, and, 63

Trekking into the interior to establish farms beyond Britain's reach, the self styled 'Afrikaners' became fine horsemen and rifle shots.

Hardy, reserved, patriarchal, the farming Afrikaners are bound by a tradition which belongs to ox wagons and horse buggies they made themselves.

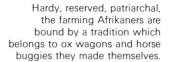

though they numbered under two hundred, they were about one sixth of the white population of the settlement. Most of the Huguenots were young; they married young, and produced large families – which is why today all over South Africa there are fresh complexioned, latin-eyed brunettes with surnames like de Plessis, du Toit, Fouché, Joubert and van Reenan (i.e. from Rouen), all chatting away in their short-clipped Afrikaans tongue.

In the meantime the farmers or Boers, to use their own word, who had been sent to grow grain by the Company, were becoming increasingly independent – especially those who lived furthest from the seat of authority. The Company gave them no help in their struggles with the natives and they learnt how to deal with the chiefs (Hottentots and later Bantu), making allies of some, bargaining – illicitly – with others, and driving away those who made raids on their cattle as the herds and flocks went further afield.

Growing wheat became unprofitable, for prices dropped as production rose. Besides, to grow wheat, one had to have farm machinery, wagons, and labor to drain and till the soil. Grain had to be transported to the

64

Carving out their farms in the veldt, the independent Afrikaners made sure they could not see the smoke of their neighbor's homestead.

nearest warehouse over long distances and unmade roads. Cattle needed less labor. Animals walked to market. Above all, pastures which lay beyond the Company's control were free.

And so by the end of the 18th century, there were two kinds of Afrikaner: those near to Cape Town, who produced wine, swilled brandy, and lived in richly endowed farms with white dovecotes and white gables – the work of imported 'Malay' craftsmen; then, up-country, there were other Afrikaners who drank substitute coffee, and smoked inferior tobacco in their long pipes. The up-country Afrikaners were bearded men, magnificent horsemen and, from beneath the broad brims of their sun hats, even more magnificent rifle shots. More primitive, less refined, with fewer possessions and more strength of character, they asked only that they should not see the smoke of their neighbor's chimney. These were the men who in the end led the revolt that turned the Afrikaners into a nation.

The English helped too, for by taking possession of the Cape in 1795, they drove the farmers northwards into almost complete isolation from the events of their own country. But they never succeeded in turning the Afrikaners into loyal subjects of the British Crown.

In the first place the Afrikaners would not allow Scottish Presbyterians or schoolmasters who hardly spoke their language to replace their own ministers and teachers. They were unwilling to submit to British judges who regarded the word of a heathen Hottentot equal to that of a Christian farmer and they resented the influence of British missionaries who set themselves up as the leaders of those they had converted. They were indignant that the British, who claimed authority over them, gave only limited support in their campaigns against natives and at times hindered their attempts to recover stolen cattle. Many of the Boer farmers were ruined during the 1830s when 39,000 slaves were freed without adequate or prompt compensation.

And so, in 1836 came the Afrikaners' exodus, the Great Trek, during which more than 10,000 men, women and children, nearly a quarter of the total white population of the Cape, left behind all their non-valuable possessions and crossed first the Orange River and, later, the Vaal further north, into the Transvaal. It was not an exodus under a single Moses. Some parties went west and found the deserts of South West Africa. Some even took the wheels off their trek wagons and slid down the steep slopes of the Drakensberg mountains through the violet shadows, past crags and waterfalls, past red hot poker flowers sprouting like rockets among the boulders to green pastures of waving grass, and beyond to the white rollers of the Indian Ocean.

For the majority it was the final break from European civilization: they were now a new people in a new land, with a single cultural inheritance, the Bible, which each family carried for religious comfort and spiritual guidance.

At the end of the Great Trek the Afrikaners, with their love of independence, formed numerous small republics. They lost and won battles against the Zulu, the Basuto (Sotho), and other tribes, and finally convinced the British that it paid to have them as friends who would earn their keep by manning the northern frontiers of Queen Victoria's South Africa.

Although the Transvaal and the Orange Free State had been granted freedom from British interference in the 1850s, the repeated efforts of the British to bring them back under control, especially with the swift growth of the diamond and gold mining industries, led eventually to the Boer Wars. The Anglo-Boer War of 1899-1902 threatened to exterminate all Afrikaners outside Cape Colony and forced peoples of the two former republics to accept what they had previously resisted – a union with the two colonies of the Cape and Natal under the British flag. But all attempts to smother the Afrikaners' language, now readily distinguishable from any other, both in vocabulary and grammar, failed, as did plans to establish new communities of British settlers who would outnumber and outvote the Afrikaners.

Afrikaans is now the national language, the language of street names and public notices: the language of officialdom. English-speaking South Africans still hold leading positions in industry and commerce but, in 1948, Field Marshal Smuts who had represented the English element in South Africa for a quarter of a century, was defeated in the general elections and the Afrikaner National Party has since enjoyed political supremacy.

But the Afrikaner's way of life is changing. He no longer scorns trade; many are in the chain-store business. Although in the countryside away from the towns a small farmer is equal to a neighbor whose farm may be much bigger, in the towns social distinctions are peeping through. Notice is taken of dress, cars, and the general standard of living. The rugby captain has replaced the big-game hunter as hero-in-chief. Above all they are becoming increasingly aware of the world beyond the borders of South Africa.

65

In spite of the rapid growth of towns and urban commerce, the roots of the political system lie with the conservative rural Afrikaner.

Peoples of Madagascar

Madagascar is a large, dramatically beautiful island 250 miles off the coast of south-east Africa. The smooth coral coastlines of the east give way to lush forests, volcanic mountain ranges and a central plateau of bare rolling moorland. Many rivers and waterfalls irrigate the plains and forests, which provide a paradise for all kinds of famous fish and animals, like the curious monkey-like lemur, tree-frogs, chameleons and many kinds of bats. Madagascar is nine hundred miles long, and roughly the size of France, Belgium and Holland put together, with a relatively minute population of only about seven million. These people, so few in number, are nevertheless so varied and their existence presents so many mysteries that they have been the subject of many learned controversies since the 16th century, when the Portuguese discovered them, and later, as French and other European travelers learnt of their existence.

Although the island is so close to Africa, its inhabitants have few close links with the African languages, races and cultures. The only definite ties which have been established are with people living several thousands of miles away in the far east of Asia, in Indonesia. All the Malagasy speak one language; few comparable areas of the African continent are held together linguistically like this. The language is divided into many dialects, but it clearly belongs to the great Malayo-Polynesian family which includes such languages as Indonesian, Malay and Maori. In their culture, too, the Malagasy clearly show their relationship with south-east Asia. The terraced rice fields in the center of Madagascar are reminiscent of Java; the remarkable second burials of Madagascar's Merina people, in which corpses of the dead are exhumed several years after death, have their parallels in Borneo; the outrigger canoes of the Vezo on the west coast are not unlike the ocean-going Polynesian canoes of the Pacific. In social organization the Malagasy of the center and east are like the peoples of Indonesia. Many of the inhabitants of the center, with their straight black hair, their light coloring and their small stature would not look foreign in the streets of Kuala Lumpur in Malaya.

Madagascar and Indonesia are definitely connected, but nobody knows how. Even the Polynesians and their cousins the Indonesians, who are famous sailors, sailing straight across the Indian Ocean would be an improbable feat. Although the currents would have helped, the fact that islands on their course, like Mauritius, were unpopulated when the Europeans landed there in the 15th century tends to undermine this hypothesis. The other possibility is that the Indonesians had at the time of their coming a series of staging posts perhaps in Ceylon, South Arabia and the East African coast and that these have now disappeared. There are suggestions of contact with Indonesian cultures in all these places; for example, African xylophones are tuned in the same way as those of Borneo. But all this evidence is flimsy, nor do we know when these migrations occurred. Yet the Indonesian element is indisputably there.

The origins of the negroid element in the Malagasy nation is perhaps even more puzzling. Probably it is basically African, but its cultural affinities are far from clear. It is easier to explain the origins of the peoples of the west coast such as the Sakalava and the Vezo or those of the south such as the Antaisaka and Antandroy, who, though their language is basically Malayo-Polynesian, are clearly linked to East Africa by aspects of their culture – the importance of cattle, and their form of royal ancestor cult particularly. Indeed there is good historical evidence of continuing contact between the west coast of Madagascar and East Africa. But the negroid element is not confined to the west and south. All along the east coast are groups of other negroid peoples living largely in the band of forest which follows the coast where they practise shifting agriculture. They are such peoples as the Betsimisaraka and Tanala and their culture can only be linked tenuously with Indonesia and not at all with Africa. How did it come about that these African-looking peoples should be the bearers of such non-African culture? We do not yet know enough about all the cultures of the East African coast to see which one they might be related to.

Although the Indonesian element, the African negroid element, and the Indonesian negroid element can all be separated, they are in fact mixed together all over Madagascar. While one element may dominate in one place, and another somewhere else, nowhere is any of these three elements completely absent. This mixture has led to a homogeneity behind the variation which has surprised all observers. It means that Malagasy culture is radically different from any other in the world.

If the origins of Malagasy culture remain much of a mystery, several more recent influences are better documented. Perhaps the most significant is the influence of the Islamic Arab and Swahili cultures which were so important along the eastern coast of Africa. The Arabs probably set up trading posts as far as Madagascar from the 8th century AD onwards but these distant Malagasy outposts were the first to get cut off in times of trouble. The clearest influence of this early Arabic contact is, strangely, not in the north but in the south-east among a group of peoples called the Antaimoro. Probably the Arabs established kingdoms in this area to escape the unwelcome sovereignty of their compatriots from the north. However when the Portuguese rounded the cape they began systematically to destroy Arab trade in the Indian Ocean and to sack isolated outposts. This process rapidly isolated Madagascar and probably the true Arabs were either killed or left. They nonetheless left behind their subjects and their slaves to carry on the little they knew of the Islamic tradition.

Today many of the descendants of these ex-subjects still claim to be Muslims though they know little of

Islamic religion, hardly ever mentioning Mohammed. But they preserve unchanged a form of Arabic script which they had adapted to Malagasy. Learned men possessed manuscript books containing family histories, odd verses from the Koran and above all astrological and medicinal information. Famous for their knowledge throughout Madagascar the Antaimoro are sought by all as doctors, diviners, and astrologers.

The Arabs also had great influence in northern Madagascar. There contact with the great Arab trading port of Africa was never lost and especially with the last remaining of these Arab settlements, the tiny archipelago of the Comoros to the north of Madagascar.

Since the Arabs the most important cultural contacts have been with Europeans. In the 17th century the French attempted to set up a colony in the far south at Fort Dauphin but this failed for various reasons. The support from France was less forthcoming and the early friendship of the Malagasy turned to hostility as the colonists tried to gain more control over them. The 18th century was a period when adventurers and pirates from America, France, Britain and Holland used Madagascar as a base to prey on trade in the Indian Ocean. Some of these pirates intermarried with the coastal peoples and are still remembered.

Most important of all, however, was the influence of British missionaries from the early 19th century onwards. This is described in the chapter on the Merina. Following the missionaries came French and British traders and others whose aim was to establish a colony. However, British and French rivalry meant that neither gained the upper hand until 1895 when the two governments reached an agreement which placed Madagascar under French influence. From 1895 to 1960 Madagascar was a colony. Then it became again an independent state, the Malagasy Republic.

Today the peoples of Madagascar can still be roughly divided into three groups: the peoples of the west coast and of the south who live in arid pasturelands interspersed by thin forest dominated by baobabs; the people of the central plateau who live in much more mountainous country with hardly any tree coverings; and the people of the east coast who inhabit the heavy tropical forest and mountainous country of that area.

Of the peoples of the west, the Antankarana are those where the influence of the Arabs is most marked. They practise a mixture of agriculture and pastoralism but what they value above all is their cattle. Cattle are a sign of wealth and the means of getting a wife and of performing the essential ceremonies in memory of the dead when the animals must be ritually slaughtered. To the south are the Tsimihety. They are strikingly unlike the other peoples of this area. They are not organized in states with kings. Instead they rely exclusively for their organization on their clans whose symbols are their family herds marked by the distinguishing patterns into which they cut the ears of their cattle. They have no elaborate religious and political traditions. Yet as a tribe they have a dynamism which has led to their taking up even more and more territory as they either push out or absorb their neighbors.

The most famous of these west coast peoples is undoubtedly the Sakalava. The word Sakalava denotes on the one hand the peoples of that name, similar to the Tsimihety to the north or the Bara to the south. They are organized in clans where the authority of the elders is paramount and where many of the most important values are linked with cattle. On the other hand the word Sakalava denotes the subjects of the kingdoms of the Sakalava princes who established large kingdoms from the 15th century onwards. They conquered agriculturalists who in the south are called Masihono; hunters and gatherers from the forest, the Mitea; and fishermen, the Vezo. They also had slaves, often of African descent, which they had either captured or bought. At the height of their glory they also attracted Islamized merchants of Arab origin and later Indians. These fascinating kingdoms, based more on the diversity of their peoples than their similarity, were united by an elaborate royal cult based on the spirits of the dead monarchs. The other peoples in this group such as the Antandroy were similar to the Sakalava and are notable for elaborate tomb carvings.

There are peoples of the central plateau: the Merina and Betsileo. Their life is dominated by irrigated rice agriculture – reflected in the very complicated social arrangements which are necessary to ensure the control of water – and by their tombs which are symbols of their families and of their ties with the soil and their ricefield. They were until the 18th century organized in small kingdoms based on fortified villages, but these became absorbed in the growing Merina power in the 19th century.

Finally there are the peoples of the east coast forest. They live in small one-room houses often standing on stilts and made of light branches and leaves. Their fields are patches of cleared forest in which they grow dry rice and bananas or sometimes maize. They cultivate such a field for a few years and then they move on. They complement their food supply by many products from the forest such as honey – which they use as a relish and also to ferment fresh water into an alcoholic concoction tasting rather like rum. Inland people catch prawns and crayfish from rivers; coastal islanders have the wealth of the sea. This eastern people obtains many roots from the ground and fruits from the trees; they even sometimes eat lemurs. Their social organization, too, seems to be governed by the forest. Their small isolated villages are traditionally very largely independent of each other and the only occasions for larger gatherings are religious, such as funerals, circumcisions or sacrifices to God and to ancestors.

Tanala
Madagascar

All along the east coast of Madagascar grow rich forests, which descend steeply from the high plateau land to the level of the sea. In the 17th century French traders who wanted to colonize these lands asked the peoples of the plateau who lived up there in the forests. 'The Tanala' they were told. What the French, and many people since, did not know is that 'Tanala' means nothing more than 'people of the forest'; and many different groups of people got their living in the damp, dense forest land. But the name Tanala stuck.

Fifty miles or so east of the Betsileo town of Abositra in southern central Madagascar the coastal forest strip is interrupted by a sort of wide step. This is the home of about 20,000 Tanala people, the Zafimaniry. The forest in their country is different from the forest inhabited by other Tanala groups, like the Betsimisaraka. It is mountainous and covered by very dense forests containing many species of trees and so much colder up there that it is not unusual to have early morning frost in July and August. There is hardly any flat ground and the Zafimaniry are often forced to cultivate their crops on hillside fields which slope as steeply as 45° or even worse. It is also, for eleven months out of twelve, sopping wet. Zafimaniry country is almost perpetually drenched by rain.

Nevertheless the Zafimaniry cultivate by the slash-and-burn method, carefully clearing and cutting down the forest, allowing it to dry – only possible in August and September – and then firing it. The fire clears the ground and the ash fertilizes the soil. They then plant a mixture of maize and climbing beans: the beans climb up the maize. In the bottom of the valleys they plant taro, a large root crop which tastes rather like chestnuts. The most arduous part of this cultivation is not, as one might think, clearing the forest, but keeping off the birds, especially parrots, when the crop is ripening. Then entire villages become deserted as everybody camps by their fields and takes turns day and night to act as human scarecrows. They do this by an ingenious device. They cover whole fields with a network of strings with all kinds of things hanging from them. This network is connected to a master rope which, when tugged, agitates the scarecrows all over the field. The parrots are so bold that they would not be frightened by anything any further away.

Moving along the paths which connect the villages is like walking down the middle of a stream. A Zafimaniry village is impressive. Perched high up on a mountain, often on a rock that dominates a vast sea of forest, hidden in the early morning clouds, mist and rain, the village is like an island in the sun from which can be seen similar islands – other villages beyond the steaming humidity. From their dominant positions in the mountains they are not only well-placed for defense; here they can avoid being flooded and swamped with liquid mud. The 30-odd houses of the village are like log cabins with the logs laid vertically instead of horizontally; four little windows are let into the wooden walls and the thresholds are raised two feet from ground level to keep the rain out. High up under the eaves are tiny windows to let out the smoke from inside, as they have no chimneys. The roof is steeply pitched and, as thatch would rot in the wet, made of flattened bamboo. But what makes these houses famous throughout Madagascar is that they are almost entirely covered by fine, low relief carvings. The walls are all covered in geometrical patterns formed by hatching. The windows and doors are decorated in different complicated geometrical patterns formed by the intersection of circles and arcs symbolically representing the sky, the daily path of the sun and the stars. Above the roof are richly decorated wooden towerlets sometimes surmounted by carvings of birds at rest: symbols of peace and harmony.

Inside the houses are simple. There is usually only one room dominated by three pillars. The head of the house uses the central pillar as a back-rest. At the south end of the room, in a slight depression in the floor, is the hearth made of three stones to support the cooking pots. All the family's belongings are arranged along shelves on the south wall, with a tidiness reminiscent of Japanese houses. The first thing a visitor would notice are the rows of maize hanging from the roof. The food has to be stored inside the house and not in the humid air outside so that the continual household fires can prevent it from rotting. But the fires turn everything inside shiny black with soot and the air is continually filled with smoke.

The wood of all the rich variety of forest trees is inestimably important to the Zafimaniry. Even four year old children can identify several hundred kinds of wood. The Zafimaniry know that certain types of wood repel insects and so are suitable for rafters. They know that other woods do not rot easily and so are good for foundations; that certain woods have a dense grain for carving and that others are supple. They know too that different woods burn at a different rate. They use tree bark to make textiles by stretching the bark to dry, then beating it and boiling the fibers into bark thread ready for spinning and weaving on small looms. These produce strips of rather stiff, scratchy cloth a foot wide and eight feet long, which is very hard wearing. Patterns are woven in by using thread dyed by bark or the leaves of other trees. Although modern imported textiles are replacing this laborious traditional method, the Zafimaniry still make clothes in times of difficulty, and shrouds always, in the old way.

They handle wood with great skill. Small boys cut down large trees all by themselves with razor sharp axes and as an almost constant occupation are forever carving their own spinning tops and other toys. The adults produce a great variety of boxes and containers and highly decorated wooden coffins which they put in their tombs in tunnels deep in the forest under isolated boulders.

This skill in handling wood has been the basis of two new sources of income with which the Zafimaniry pay their taxes and the indirect expenses of the churches and

(Right) Tanala villages are almost permanently shrouded in thick cloud and mist. Fighting the rotting damp is a constant necessity.

(Far right) Before a circumcision begins, several villages who have gathered to celebrate it are entertained by local singers.

(Top) Tanala girls pound maize outside a hut built from vertically placed logs – an architecture unique to these inhabitants of dense forests.

Tanala Madagascar

Tanala woven bark cloth is stiff and scratchy and largely superseded by imported cloth. But it is very hardwearing and unbeatable for shrouds.

During the initiation ritual villagers attack the boy's hut with hands and spears; often the hut is damaged or even knocked down.

Windows, ornately carved with symbolic designs, also function as chimneys, letting out the smoke from the constantly burning fires.

(Middle) Before circumcision village youths chase a bull and kill it. Soon they will take it in the initiate's hut, and make him dance all night.

schools that Christian missionaries are introducing. The Zafimaniry have recently been producing tourist goods, little boxes, statuettes or chains which are sold in Tananarive. And for two or three months of the year young men sell their unequaled skill as foresters.

The forest is also for the Zafimaniry a source of their precious honey. They place hives in the trees in which swarms of wild bees may settle, and make honey which can be collected once a year. The collectors make a fire of moss so that the acrid smoke will drive away the bees. Then they climb the tree, take the honey and put it in the great wooden containers which hold up to thirty gallons. Honey-collecting is a big industry among the Zafimaniry. They use honey as a relish with maize or taro, as their only sweetener, and as the food which must be offered to honor any stranger. Honey can also be distilled to produce a kind of bitter-tasting rum.

Other produce of the forest includes, as a major source of protein, the many crayfish and freshwater crabs which live in the streams. Nevertheless gathering shell-fish is strictly limited by taboo: they must not be sold. The untransformed products of nature belong to all and to sell them would be to abuse this shared resource.

Zafimaniry family life is in some ways very like that of urban Europeans. It is rare to find large families of many generations and married brothers and sisters, as is common in other parts of Madagascar, and children leave their parents when they marry. After betrothal they are allowed, very discreetly, to have sexual relations together. The youngest child or the last to marry tends to stay with his elderly parents. When he has married he takes over his parents' household, and gradually what little there is to inherit.

Apart from marriage, the most important event in a boy's life is his initiation, marked here, as everywhere else in Madagascar, by circumcision. Little boys are circumcised around the age of two or three to indicate their separation from the woman-centered world of the house to the nature-centered world of manhood symbolized by the strength of rushing water and of powerful animals like bulls. A Zafimaniry circumcision ceremony begins when the people of several villages assemble at the boy's home. There follows a kind of corrida when the young men of the village chase a bull around the village, kill it, then place its carcass in the north-east corner of the house. The boy is danced before the carcass all night until a group of young men rush out of the village carrying a gourd and fighting as they go – living symbols of the continuing flow of life. They scoop pure and strength-giving water from a waterfall in the forest then mark their faces with chalk, a symbol of purity, drink a lot of rum and come back armed with spears and sticks. They charge back to the young boy's house, attacking it with their hands, with their feet and their spears, so fiercely that they sometimes knock it down altogether. Then they place the water they brought back from the waterfall in the

north-east corner of the house. The men and youths now make a great din shouting 'He is a man, he is a man' as a specialist performs the circumcision operation. Then the water is poured over the boy – who is now a man.

No Zafimaniry – man or woman – is really an adult, however, until he has produced a child. Until then his advice will not be heeded, he will not be able to initiate agricultural work, and he will be last to be served at a meal. With the birth of a child his status changes dramatically: he loses his old name and is henceforth always called 'father of . . .' or in the case of a woman 'mother of . . .' To call a person who has borne children by his personal name would be deliberately to insult him.

The climate and living conditions encourage infections which make childbirth very dangerous and special precautions are taken to protect them. The mother usually returns for the birth of her child to her mother's house and is attended by the women of the village. Soon after her delivery her attendants gather to purify her by putting clay on her, and to congratulate her and bring presents for the child. They then take the umbilical cord and bury it in a field if the child is a girl, but in a beehive if it is a boy. In the house they construct another tiny house of mats and bamboos in which the mother can just about sit with her child and in which they remain for six months. This is done to keep the mother warm and out of draughts and also means that the mother stays away from her husband and is not expected to work until she and the child have become strong.

There is no definite overall political organization which unites the Zafimaniry. Indeed their remoteness in the forest is partly the result of having avoided the power of the Betsileo kings and subsequently the Merina and then the French government. Each village is independent and within the village there is no formal political structure. The respect in which the elders of the village are held is, however, enough to maintain the strictest control. Their authority is marked by such things as their precedence in speechmaking and where they sit in the house. Although it is a function of their authority to settle disputes they never act petulantly and in giving their judgements they display almost excessive humbleness. It is enough that they have spoken and it is impossible to stay in the village without their judgement.

Order and mutual respect are nowhere more evident than in Zafimaniry formal greetings. When a man meets another he has not seen for a long time he will greet him in an elaborate speech when he must outline everything of importance that has passed since they last met. Then the man who has been so addressed must repeat what the first has said almost word for word to show his respect and concern. Only after this feat of memory will he say what he has done during the same period. This too the first must duly repeat. Such a formal greeting may last for hours. It is an impressive display of manners and mutual concern.

71

Villagers around Lac Sacré
believe these crocodiles are
their ancestors, transformed
thus because they refused
water to a thirsty passer-by.

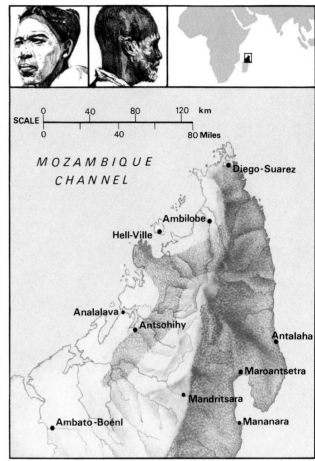

SCALE

| 0 | 40 | 80 | 120 | km |

| 0 | 40 | | 80 Miles |

MOZAMBIQUE
CHANNEL

Diego-Suarez

Ambilobe

Hell-Ville

Analalava

Antsohihy

Antalaha

Maroantsetra

Mandritsara

Mananara

Ambato-Boénl

The northern tip of the great backbone of mountains that sweeps through Madagascar from end to end is known as the Ankara range. Here in the mountains and in the surrounding foothills and coastal plains is the home of some 38,000 Antankarana, one of the most elusive and little known of all Malagasy peoples.

The Antankarana's heritage, like all Malagasys', is derived from several waves of colonizers; Indonesians, Africans, Arabs, local Merina and French.

The Antankarana, together with the Sakalava, are among the few Madagascan peoples to use outrigger canoes, exact replicas of those in which the Indonesians are thought to have crossed the Indian Ocean during the first millenium AD. No-one knows the exact route those 73

Antankarana Madagascar

(Bottom) After the bull is slaughtered, water is poured over it from the Lake, which is sacred and allegedly has magical properties.

Village women prepare for the sacrifice of a bull to feed the crocodiles and make them intercede with the ancestors on behalf of the sick.

74

The slaughtered animal is cut up, and the pieces are thrown into the lake to lure the crocodiles out onto the rocks which surround it.

(Center) The crocodile is tempted from the water. Once its appetite is whetted, it will follow the trail of meat the villagers have prepared.

A villager waits for the crocodiles to appear, tempted by the smell of blood and flesh. The further they come ashore, the better.

brave seamen took but their sailing skill has been handed down through the ages, for the coastal Antankarana are considered excellent sailors and fishermen. Indonesian influence is evident too in their language which is not African but belongs to the Malayo-Polynesian group.

From 1,000 AD onwards Bantu-speaking Africans crossed eastwards over the 250 miles of water to Madagascar. The Antankarana, tall and well-built with rich brown skin, are the most negroid-looking of all Malagasys. Some however, show distinct Arab ancestry, dating from the 12th century when Arab traders persisted down the East African coast eventually reaching Madagascar where they established trading towns, forcing the Indonesians inland. During the great Merina expansion of the 18th century some Antankarana fled westwards and intermarried with the Sakalava. They became Muslims. Those who stayed in their homeland accepted Merina rule, and adopted some Merina customs. Later they came under the rule of the French who brought industry and large towns to Madagascar. Today many Antankarana work in the factories of Diégo Suarez and Vohémar in the north-east of the island. Those living in the more rural areas are cattle-breeders and fishermen, living in simple dwellings and worshipping their ancestors.

About thirty miles from Diégo Suarez lies a volcanic lake, known as the Lac Sacré. In this lake there are fearsome, large-jawed crocodiles. Elsewhere in Madagascar crocodiles have been ruthlessly exploited for their skins which command enormous prices in western markets. But in the Lac Sacré they are numerous. The people who live near the lake are thought to believe in a legend which tells of a stranger who long ago visited the village that stood where the lake now lies. The stranger asked the villagers for a drink of water but they all refused his request save one kindly old woman. On the stranger's instructions she left the village – and wisely too – for a catastrophe struck in the form of a great flood which drowned the village and all its inhabitants. The inhabitants are believed to have turned into crocodiles.

It is claimed that the lake-side villagers of today believe the crocodiles are their ancestors. If someone is ill or a woman finds herself barren the crocodiles are called forth from the lake to intercede with the god, Zanahary, on behalf of the afflicted person. This is not as hard as it sounds. The blood of a ceremonial bull, or zebu, is thrown into the lake at the shore's edge. When, smelling the blood in the water, a crocodile appears a crowd of people standing on the shore play drums and wind instruments and women chant. At the same time warm zebu meat is left on the shore's edge and the crocodile is enticed out of the water and up the shore by further strategically placed lumps of flesh. The further the crocodile comes on land the more effective their intercessions are believed and the better the chances of the afflicted individual's recovery.

For the duration of the ceremony, the village women chant and pray, and put before the animals their requests for health and prosperity.

Vezo Madagascar

The Vezo fishermen of the west coast of Madagascar are one of the less known peoples of the world. Very little has been written about them in English. They have always been isolated, living in small semi-nomadic groups behind the sand dunes and usually marrying among themselves. They live on the coastal edge of the vast tract of country inhabited and largely ruled by Sakalava peoples that covers almost a quarter of Madagascar. But though the Vezo language has Sakalava elements, and the Vezo have always traded with the Sakalava, exchanging dry fish for Sakalava grain, they are not a Sakalava people and have until the arrival of Christian missionaries in the 19th century kept themselves apart. Their differences persist. The legends and religion of the Vezo are peculiar to them. Despite the slight Arab influence on the west coast, the Vezo are clearly an African people with almost no Arab blood: they have very dark skin, tall, well-built bodies, flat noses, large lips and woolly hair. They are clearly of a negroid type, and hold themselves proudly with reserved expressions and undemonstrative manners.

Traditionally they wear a *salaka* or *sikiny* round their hips, a narrow cloth band of dyed cotton which men and women drape round themselves in different ways. Vezo women used to leave their breasts bare but now do so increasingly rarely. They also wear the *lamba,* something worn over almost all Madagascar – 2¾ yards of white cloth which is wrapped and folded, rather like a cross between a shawl and a toga. Some wear brightly colored head cloths, wrapped intricately round their heads; these are often colored blood red, and are rarely washed. They dip them in beef fat which makes them rainproof and warmer. But it is probably more traditional to oil and part the hair and plait it into two or more buns on either side of the head. The art of *tabake* by which their faces are decorated with spots and lines in white and yellow ointment is very important to Vezo women. Sorcerers or the women themselves apply a paste of a kind of white soil mixed with water, scented plants and the grated roots of dye-producing plants like saffron with great skill to women's faces, then leave it to dry and stick to the skin. They draw various arabesques and slanting stripes, producing a very dramatic effect. *Tabake* is therapeutic – sometimes pregnant women use it – and it is supposed to soften and beautify the skin, much as western face-packs and creams are supposed to improve the skin.

Both men and women until recently still tattooed themselves, especially on their faces. The craftsman drew a design on the skin in a paste of grease and water, and pricked it out with a needle or possibly a cactus spine if there were any cacti left in his country. He rubbed charcoal and powder from burnt mace into the bleeding tattooed parts and waited for scars to form. These fall off to reveal a bluish tattoo, which usually faded during a lifetime. They had all kinds of designs, asymetrically arranged: stars, spots, long streaks, hieroglyphic signs.

Off the south-west coast
of Madagascar a lonely Vezo
fisher boy symbolizes the
isolation and independence
of his little-known people.

Vezo Madagascar

The Vezo hack their fishing
canoes out of the trunks of
local trees. As tools they
use home-manufactured axes
with iron cutting heads.

Setting out before dawn
Vezo fishermen hunt for sea
turtles in boats distinguished
by square and prominent
outriggers.

(Top) In the face of frequent
storms and high winds, Vezo
vessels are rimmed with
wooden pegs to make them
more flexible and enduring.

They could be all over a man's or woman's back, front, arms or face; they could be of crocodiles and animals, wheels and sun emblems. Men usually had a circumflex tattooed over each eye. Tattooing showed virility and force in men, the corresponding virtues in women. Often women had their breasts and necks tattooed.

Their other still flourishing embellishment is jewelry. Pearls have magical powers and are sometimes worn; otherwise necklaces and bracelets are of bead and shell. Sometimes, but only rarely, like the Sakalava they wear gold and silver, and their women wear ornaments in the right nostril which they copied from the Arabs. They live in semi-nomadic groups along the western coast on the shores of the fitful Mozambique channel under the suzerainty of the Sakalava. Their lives are dictated by fishing – both sea fishing and fresh water fishing in the rivers that run to the sea, as for example in the River Onilahy.

Nothing is more important to the Vezo fishermen than their light and swift outriggers, which are made from dug-out tree trunks. These are of two types. There are small fishing boats called *laka firangua,* and larger ocean-going ones *(laka ki barua)* which are for deep water fishing and turtle hunting. The rich also have transport boats, and some are built for sale. The boats belong to those who sail them. All the boats have wooden outriggers built out from either side. The sails are square and made from coarse cloth, and attached by four cords to the canoe. The Vezo take aboard with them unattached oars, shaped like spades, and provisions for long journeys, taking care, however, not to take food that is forbidden, and might cause disaster.

A lot of magic surrounds boats and sailing. The Vezo carve the prows in different ways for varying types of boats. Turtle hunting boats have prows carved in flowing abstract shapes like turned-back goats' horns, and these have to be sprinkled with blood and charmed in various ways to appease the spirits of the water and ensure a good catch of turtle. Most boats are very fast and can travel at ten miles an hour. They are stable but, in the squalls that often attack the fishing fleets, they can easily be overturned, and the bravery of fishermen balancing on the outriggers and leaning out to the waves to right the boats is very impressive. To take such enormous risks would be quite impossible if the Vezo did not take magic precautions before setting out, or if they did not wait for favorable winds.

Sea turtles are good to eat and plentiful, and in some places form an important part of the Vezo's diet. Some are oval and plump. Some are thin and flat. They come up in the early morning to sleep on the surface of the sea when it is smooth. The fishermen go out at this time, as quietly as possible so as not to wake them. They catch them in many ways. Harpooning is not regarded as a very prestigious method, but nevertheless, it is spectacular. The fishermen cautiously approach with a twelve-foot harpoon with an iron barb and 200 or 300 yards of rope attached. When the turtle is struck it dives down at once. The fisherman hangs on to the rope and dives down with it, staying underwater for a very long time by human standards. Turtles caught differently must be killed in different and appropriate ways. For example, a harpooned turtle must be killed in the sea. Then it is brought ashore where the whole village has gathered on the beach to feast. Nobody must bring anything from a house to the spot. The animal must be wrenched open in front of an altar, cut in pieces and severed with knives and implements belonging to the boat. It must also be cooked in seawater and no left-over meat can be taken into a Vezo house. These and other ancestral customs must be observed for otherwise the turtles will disappear from the sea.

The Vezo of the north-west coast know a fish called *hamby* which can grow almost as big as a man's thigh. It has a dorsal fin like a brush, covered with sticky fluid which catches smaller fish on it. When the Vezo catch a *hamby* they keep it for a while in an underwater cage, feeding it with cooked rice or small fish, and when they want to go fishing they tie the *hamby's* tail to a 'lead' of stout string and follow it in a canoe. The *hamby* will then catch fish on its sticky dorsal fin, which the villagers then detach and eat themselves, restricting the unfortunate *hamby* to a smaller and less interesting diet than it would have in its natural state.

The Vezo catch other fish with rods or nets, and usually eat them whole, often without shelling or skinning them, but observing various customs. If they are on an expedition of several days they sleep on the shore behind shelters made from the mast and sails of their boats, though they have permanent village homes made of wood and banana leaves.

Their homes are built on top of the sand dunes, or in little hollows at the bottom of the inland slopes of the dunes. They are carefully arranged in parallel lines and in family groups. Grandparents, parents and children all live together in one family group in an area enclosed by a fence of mangrove wood. The more senior men live in the western part of the area. And the strip of land on the western side going down to the shore and the sea itself falls under the domination of the family patriarch. The family has what amounts to a small private beach; and it is here that they embark in their outriggers, or put up shrines for the ceremony of eating turtles, and where they actually finish building their boats. On the eastern side of the family area, where the women and girls live, there are altars for communication with the supernatural, and, as this is the inland side, cultivated land, and water wells. Strangers have to stay at a special sandy place reserved for them at the extreme south-west of the village, whereas family relations can stay on the sand dune in the strip of land belonging to the family to which they are related.

79

Vezo Madagascar

The Vezo smoke or dry
fish to feed themselves
through the wet season,
and also to sell for grain
to inland peoples.

The fishing season corresponds roughly with the dry season, after which it stops for the year. Against this time the Vezo dry and smoke fish which they exchange with inland Sakalava peoples for maize, manioc or sorghum. Some Vezo peoples grow their own simple crops, and gather bananas. They depend on inland peoples for fibers with which to make lines and nets. They themselves have highly developed techniques of spinning thread, which is a job that only the women do, though men make the actual fishing nets and lines. When the Vezo go inland to trade they leave the dunes and country of spiny dry vegetation and go upstream to a fertile country of birds and streams and magnificent sunsets. There are crocodiles in the rivers and kingfishers, black parrots and green pigeons among wild ducks and teal. Sometimes there are groups of flamingos. They dry and powder shrimps for use as a savory with rice, though for some Vezo it is *fady,* or forbidden, to mix fish with land produce or milk.

Food taboos are endless. Cooking the head and feet of an animal in one pan makes you die young. Singing as you eat makes your teeth long. Peeling a banana with your teeth makes you poor. And if you eat fallen bananas you risk killing your father. Taking lemons and oranges with you on a fishing trip means you will have no cattle. And stealing fish causes leprosy. Observing ancestral customs and *fady* is important in other things than food: it is forbidden to kill certain birds, like the one that announces bad weather, or the lark that protects the ancestral tombs.

The *fady* are a set of prohibitions, part of a wide-reaching system of magic and divination and religion that concerns natural forces and tries to harness them to the Vezo's interests. Practices differ from tribe to tribe, depending on various ways of life and natural resources. In the Morombe region diviners practise augury (*sikidy*) for clients, charging fees in cash or kind. He throws plenty of sand from a bottle on tamarind seeds. Rather as if he were reading tea leaves the diviner discerns the future from the patterns in which the sand and seeds fall. If the destiny looks bad he wipes it away with a guinea fowl's feather; tortoise bones are also auspicious. If it is good the diviner wraps up the sand in pieces of material and gives them to his client to keep as talismen. He is able to invoke spirits by using a mirror. He writes down successful or enigmatic *sikidy* in a special and often well-thumbed sign language slightly resembling the magical writing of the Antaimoro, which is partly Arabic.

There are many healing charms and medicines mostly made from wood and plants, against rheumatism, headaches, and especially women's headaches – just as a large part of the atonement ritual called *sandratsi* centers around women's fertility. Both in prayer and in spells, incense and incense-burners are used to drive away evil spirits. For everyday personal use the Vezo have necklaces made of beads which drive evil spirits away with their horrible smell, love philters which are particularly in demand, and fish whose smell when burning brings back an unfaithful wife. The Vezo carve all kinds of talismen, carefully and intricately shaped from pearls, copper and zebra's horns.

It may be because they have always been remote that some Vezo groups have preserved their practices and beliefs despite the efforts of Christian missionaries to convert all Madagascar. The *sandratsi* rites, which lay emphasis on the appeasement of gods as well as on the fertility of women, are the most important Vezo ceremony. The whole tribe or village draws together round the white painted wooden stilt-house, roughly equivalent to a European parish church, called *anjomba* which means 'house of birds'. It faces north-west and is square and decorated, with crenellated windows and roof. In the west side is a huge stool-shaped edifice which reaches the floor level. At the east a sacred tree is planted. Inside are various ritual objects: incense, seaweed, coral, glass beads strung on the cords that the Vezo fishermen appropriately call the Thread of Life. There is also rum and local earth which has great significance. In the ceremony the Vezo plead to the spirits and superior gods

81

Vezo women are socially inferior to men, walk behind them and do most household chores. Girls conform to this from a tender age.

for survival for the next year, for good catches, for forgiveness for unacceptable behavior and for violating *fady* and above all for fertility. The *anjomba* master calls the whole village group around to chant and sing prayers, and they do the placatory bird dance, which looks like an imitation of a maddened sea gull. They drink heavily and become entranced or possessed. Of the many sculptures for religious or magic purposes which the Vezo make, in this particular ceremony they use a woman figure carved in wood. From an abstract traditional shape she has developed into a crude figure with breasts and, since French colonization, she wears a French sailor's beret. She must be placed at the east of the *anjomba*. During the ceremony illness and infertility will pass from live women into her. The master of ceremonies sprinkles everyone with holy water from the sea, and a privileged person makes a sacrifice of an ox. He may later become a mouthpiece for a god and speak the god's mind.

Apart from the *vorombe* spirit in the form of a great bird the Vezo believe in other distinct superhuman beings. The *Topandrano* is the master of the water, and if you meet him at sea you have to dip money in the water saying 'This is for you God. Let us come safely onto dry land'. Some Vezo peoples believe his role is played by the goddess *Apelamananisa* and sometimes you have to put rum into the water to get a good catch. Stories about the god's caprice or favor are the basis of most Vezo songs and legends, and especially the stories told to children to keep them awake before supper. In one story three little girls go out fishing in a small canoe. The spirits of the water become displeased with them, and soon a great white bird swoops down, and carries one little girl away. The other two, very frightened, paddle home as fast as they can, and tell their people who pray and sing to the *varombe* to relent. To their amazement and great joy the little girl is brought back unharmed to her parents, and the whole village then celebrates and makes offerings to the spirits to keep their good will.

Like most Malagasy the Vezo attach great importance to funerals and to the existence of souls after death. They believe the dead look favorably on the living so long as their corpses have been respected. This means decent burial, traditionally in elaborate and fantastically carved wooden tombs not far from the village: some names, especially chief's names, become taboo after death and must never be mentioned. The Vezo do not go to

82

Vezo tribesmen and their
Mahafaly neighbors challenge
each other in *ringe* matches,
a form of wrestling peculiar
to the region.

The Vezo fishermen never keep
cattle: this ox belongs to
their neighbors and virtual
overlords, the Sakalava,
with whom they trade fish.

83

Trying to keep their
children awake before
supper, the Vezo gather
to tell tales and play
games they devise themselves.

Vezo children like
energetic pastimes. Besides
competitive sports and games
they often play crueller
games like grasshopper fights.

cemeteries to pay their respects however. They go only for burials. The craftsmanship of their tomb carving was highly developed and used to be a matter of great pride. But now the practice has almost completely died out and cemeteries are very plain, though it is possible, here and there, to find some laid out in the old way, and these have a peculiarly eerie, intense atmosphere.

Respect for the dead is part of a great respect for family and group life. Families are close and very proud of their homes and the very soil on which they live, which is evident from its use in religious ceremonies. Women have a position inferior to men and often are not allowed to eat with them. In cattle herding areas women are not considered suitable for the noble task of milking cows, which is a man's job. They must go to find water from their brackish seashore wells and they are expected to carry burdens for their men and usually to walk behind them. The Vezo have many children, though in the past they used to kill those born on days which were *fady*; often two days a week were taboo. A woman in labor gives birth in a special hut, squatting on her heels and assisted by relations. As among the Tanala the placenta is thought important and has to be buried north of the mother's house (or south in the case of a girl baby). Uncomfortably soon after the birth the mother must purify herself in the sea or nearby river but she can rest for a long period after parturition. She must take care not to look in a mirror or the baby will be ill and if she kisses the baby's ears it will become deaf. In fact the Vezo did not know what kissing was until they learnt it from Europeans. They prefer to show affection by rubbing noses or cheeks. When friends and relations come to congratulate the father they must not ask to see the mother and her baby as to do so would bring misfortune. They bring him money to buy fresh-water shrimps which have many magic powers and will make the baby grow strong and healthy.

Children – especially girls, who have less time to play than their brothers – learn to share their parents' work at an early age. In some groups women go fishing – as in the folk tale about the three little girls – but usually they do domestic jobs, leaving their brothers to some rather ferocious games like wrestling or torturing small animals. Little boys tear off grasshoppers' wings and set them to fight each other. There are other games too for the time before dinner. The Vezo eat late, at about eight pm European time, and they believe that children must not sleep before dinner, so families play games and tell stories or make shadows in the evening sun with their hands. They would not describe the time of day with a number. The hour before eight is called 'the time when children play'. Between two and three in the morning is 'the time when frogs croak', and midday is 'when the day splits in two'. The Vezo have languages that are full of images, and very musical, in which to express the richness of their traditions and myths.

In the past Vezo graves were decorated with exotic carvings, but the art is now lost, and these wooden statues are the last of their kind.

After a busy market-day these Vezo women make their way home, fighting one of the frequent sandstorms with unsold wares on their heads.

Merina
Madagascar

In Merina legends stories of
heroic kings are entwined
with tales about origins of
rice species and cooking.
Rice stands for honor and life.

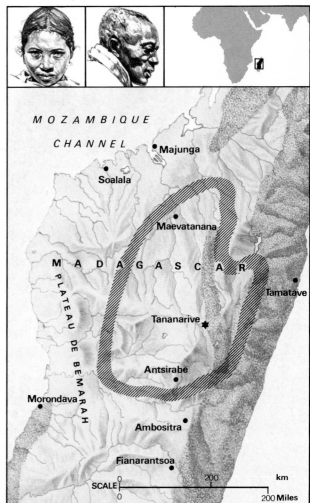

At the time of the French conquest of Madagascar in 1895, the Merina ruled almost the whole of that vast island from their capital at Tananarive. They were a unified people who had been brought together by a prince called Andrianampoinimerina, which meant 'prince in the heart of the land of Merina'. He had overwhelmed the Merina's neighbors and, as time passed, the Merina were strengthened by firearms brought by early European visitors. But the Christian faith also brought by Europeans was not accepted so readily. Many Merina were martyred because of their conversion to this new faith. When eventually a Merina queen was converted, however, Christianity became the symbol of their nationhood. Soon the Merina, from a position of strength, were sending ambassadors to France and England and to many other European countries. Their queen exchanged gifts with Queen Victoria. Their laws were printed on royal printing presses and their army was dressed in European uniforms. Europe was already beginning to exert many influences on the ways of 87

The Merina play their music on the *valiha*, a bamboo pipe with strings along it which they pluck to produce a tune.

(Bottom) In 1777 the first European visitor discovered that Merina blacksmiths used smelting furnaces just like those used in Indonesia.

Merina have no use for garlic, but this woman has learnt to grow it and sells it to Europeans in Tananarive market.

the Merina.

Of all the peoples of Madagascar the Merina are the most recognizably of Indonesian origin. In the highest social groups they are often as light-skinned as sun-tanned Europeans. Their hair is straight and black and their stature slight. Others by contrast have typically African features with dark skin and frizzy hair. Most are in between these two extremes. But perhaps the most characteristic feature of their appearance today is their willing acceptance of European styles of dress, although certain features prevail as particularly valued signs of Malagasy culture. The most striking of these is the white stole which Merina women always wear around their shoulders and in which they, and when necessary their husbands, carry small babies completely covered up so that they seem like a hump on the parent's back. On weekdays this stole is made of ordinary material but on Sundays it is of a traditional natural silk of great beauty. Also of great significance as part of the woman's dress are the ubiquitous parasols which they carry, and their hair, plaited so elaborately that it can take several hours. Today men dress in a traditional way only in the country, where they wear a long blouse and trousers made of pajama-like materials with long pieces of cloth draped around their shoulders and falling down to the ground,

A Merina prince established Tananarive as his capital and built his palace on the hill. In spite of French occupation it is still the Merina capital.

reminiscent of Roman senators' togas. They top these distinctive clothes with hats, which they are forever buying and which almost every Merina wears. Some are in the traditional style with broad brims; others are completely new in style like a type of straw hat, which became very popular at the time of the moon landings. These were the Apollo XII hats, said to have been worn by American astronauts.

Many Merina towns and villages have also been susceptible to western influence. Many have buildings in European styles, some of which go back to the beginning of the century – like the houses which followed the fashion for South African-type balustrades supported on four columns. Nonetheless there are traditional buildings everywhere. In Tananarive this mixture is accentuated by the way the town is dominated by two palaces: one for the Queen, the other for her spouse, the 'prime minister', where, inside a European-style shell which dates from the 19th century, traditional wooden buildings, large versions of old Merina houses, are encased.

In spite of the number of modern buildings there are still many traditional and picturesque villages. Merina villages often nestle on the brow of a hill, surrounded by several very deep concentric moats. There is just one gate by which you can enter the village, firmly closed in the 89 past by a stone disc about 15 feet in diameter which was rolled back with great effort each morning and evening. In the village the houses are the same red color as the earth of which they are made. They rise narrow and tower-like on two storeys topped by a steeply pitched roof covered with thatch. All doors and windows face west. Inside everything is organized on the basis of the notion that the north-east corner is the holiest direction associated with ancestors. The hearth is to the south but water, which is thought of as slightly purer, is stored to the east of it. The head of the family sleeps in the north-east of the house. South and west of him sleep his wife, then his children, and finally his servants, their heads all pointing in the same direction. In the north-east corner itself is kept a bunch of rice, the first fruits of the preceding years, with the family medicines and charms. When a son is married, it is in this sacred north-east corner that the dowry is piled up. At circumcision the plants symbolic of fertility will be stored here. And here, when there is death in the family, the corpse is surrounded by mourners. This principle of orientation governs all life inside the house.

As well as its houses, every village has at least one church – Protestant, Catholic or both. Since the beginning of the 19th century there has been great rivalry between British congregationalist and French catholic missionaries. Today, the Merina are among the most Christian people in the world. But what really dominates the Merina village and indeed all the surrounding countryside are the Merina family tombs. All travelers to Madagascar remark how large, important and permanent these tombs are, compared with the houses of the living. A Merina stone tomb normally costs about ten times the cost of a house. Some of the stones are massive slabs, ten feet square or more. The top part of the tomb is overground, but the tomb chamber itself is underground and can hold many corpses. The entire edifice is today often covered by cement, decorated by balustrades or arcades which owe something to traditional folk art and much to various European styles, often of the last century. Many villages which have long lost all their inhabitants maintain a ghostly existence by the presence of tombs which outlast houses. In these, the descendants of people who dwell in other living villages will ultimately be buried. It is by their permanence that the tombs are so important. They are perpetual ties for Merina groups within their territory and their ricefields. They manifestly outlast the passage of generations. To have a place in a tomb is to show that a man belongs to a particular group, and therefore has a particular rank. Not to have a tomb is to be nobody; to be, in all probability, the descendant of slaves (although even they too are now building tombs); to have no family. To have a tomb means that one's ancestors were associated with the glorious history of kings and princes. It is the only true warranty of being a Merina. It is a concrete demonstration that a man has legitimate rights of access to rice fields. And every Merina village has its associated rice fields.

Following their early contact with European missionaries the Merina became well educated in western learning and rapidly rose in the French administration. They became traders and businessmen, took advantage of higher education, often in France, and became doctors, dentists, lawyers and engineers. They adapted their traditional love of literature. The importance of oratory, the ability to express important matters of the day in a traditional way, well illustrated with proverbs and historical allusions, is still a valued Merina skill. And there is an amazing number of newspapers and books written by Merina authors both in Malagasy and in French. In the past this literary ability also involved poetry. This was sometimes heroic but more often it was intimate, dealing with domestic and personal matters in a half ironical, half affectionate way.

Still where the Merina heart lies is in the rice fields, the basis of Merina life, of Merina social organization and of all Merina values. Most Merina are still peasant cultivators of rice. The Merina phrase 'to eat a meal' literally means to eat rice, for a meal is basically rice in which all other elements are grouped together as 'rice

(Top) Merina men and boys prepare the fields for rice planting by running cattle around them to churn up the muddy, flooded soil.

The north-east corner is the holiest in Merina homes, and where the head of the house sleeps. All doors and windows face the west.

Mountain slopes have to be
terraced to keep up the
water level in the fields
where Merina women
grow their sacred rice.

After a Merina betrothal the man gives his bride clothes and money. In return her family present him with a dowry of household goods.

(Bottom) At one time Merina girls were obliged to marry for inheritance, to keep rice fields within the nearby group of villages.

flavorings' whether they are meat, green vegetables, fish, potatoes or tins of sardines. A poor man is a man who does not have rice, but has to make do with such famine-breakers as manioc or maize. There is an enormous vocabulary devoted simply to distinguishing the types of rice by species and to differentiating the stages of growth. The stories of the heroic kings of the past are all intertwined with stories about the origin of certain rice cooking techniques or certain rice fields. When Andrianampoinimerina wanted to say that he considered the whole of Madagascar as his, he said 'The sea is the boundary of my rice field.' The cultivation of rice begins in November when the seedlings are sown in tiny rice fields. The seedlings grow, spreading bright green quilts over the land which is elsewhere dusty and brown. Then, around the capital, the larger fields are plowed as soon as the rains begin, in preparation for transplanting; but in other areas a simpler method is used. A herd of cattle is driven onto the flooded field. The men shout and sing, chasing the cattle before them, so that their hoofs break up the hard soil into a liquid mud ready for the transplanting. Young men trying to prove their manhood jump on the backs of terrified bulls and hold on until either their strength or that of the bull gives out. Then the laborious task of transplanting begins. It is backbreaking work, for the women must finish it by December if the rice is to have long enough to grow. By June, the rice is ready for harvesting and the men are out in the fields with long straight sickles. They then stack the stalks ready for threshing. This is done either by beating on a stone or, more simply, by spreading the crop on the ground so that the cattle trample it and separate the rice from the straw. The rice is then stored unhusked, so that insects do not destroy it, in basket-lined underground pits. This means that every morning, and sometimes twice a day, women and children must winnow and pound it in front of their houses in the massive mortars which are so characteristic of Merina villages. Only then is it ready to cook. This means boiling without any seasoning, since rice is too sacred to be polluted by any other foods.

Groups of Merina villages, centered around nearby rice fields, form the basic traditional unit of Merina society. The inhabitants of these villages were all members of a group rather like a Scottish clan. In the past the group's members were represented by their leaders at the Merina court. The king organized all relations between groups and everyone's status within his group corresponded to these arrangements. The unity of a group came primarily, however, from their joint inherited ownership of the rice lands on which they depended as their ancestors did before them. To keep their lands within the group, the Merina insisted that all their daughters married members of their own group, so that no alien could ever be an heir to their rice lands. Marriages like these were often described as a 'closing of the breach in the wall' or as an 'inheritance not going away marriage'. A marriage did not have the usual significance of giving away a daughter; in fact the Merina called it an exchange of 'a male crab for a female crab', creatures for which the differences of sex are irrelevant. The groom gave money to the family of the bride and new clothes to her. But her family had to give him a dowry of bedding and household things of equal value.

The Merina are often described as having a form of ancestor worship – a misleading statement today since they are all orthodox Christians, apart from minor beliefs in nature sprites and ghosts which they themselves do not take very seriously. The importance of tombs and the importance of linking the living to the previous generations buried within the tombs has, however, meant that several ceremonies have developed. Although being placed in a tomb is of paramount social importance, the time of death may well not be suitable for such a great ceremony: death often comes unexpectedly. Also a ceremony is expensive, and it can take a long time to assemble the whole family of the deceased, who may live anywhere in Madagascar. And then Merina society is so mobile these days that people often die far away from their ancestral homes. So they are buried temporarily where they die and later, when the body is reduced to a skeleton and the preparations are completed, they can be returned to their ancestral home and the ancestral tomb. The corpse is exhumed and reburied, properly, in its tomb. In the season when these second burial ceremonies take place one can see along all the roads of Madagascar, processions of relatives preceded by a flag returning the corpses of their kinsmen to their tomb. It is a time of family reunion, in a practical and in a spiritual sense.

Many people gather for the opening of the tomb. These second funerals are the largest of all Merina feasts and ceremonies. Nevertheless these grand public occasions are, for the people most closely concerned, intensely personal affairs. Close relatives are frightened and shocked as the corpse is exhumed. Then comes a period for piety towards the dead. A eulogy is spoken of the dead while his corpse lies wrapped in a mat on the laps of his close female relatives, followed by offerings of new, multicolored silk shrouds from each of the dead man's many descendants. Then comes the most surprising element of the entire ceremony. The relatives have to dance with the corpse on their shoulders and have to maltreat it and joke with it. This is so that they may be aware that they are in fact dealing with nothing but a corpse while it is being reintegrated with its group. It has no individuality but is only part of the group. It will be reincorporated with its group in the tomb in the land of its ancestors. Here it will be supported by preceding generations and will support future generations. The women of the group grab at bits of the mats in which the corpses were wrapped to increase their fertility. Death in this way is transformed into a ritual of continuing life.

Merina ancestral tombs are more expensive and enduring than Merina homes. They testify to the dead man's rank and social status.

(Bottom) The dead are often buried temporarily. Later, when the family has assembled, bodies are exhumed for reburial in the ancestral tomb.

Peoples of Mauritius

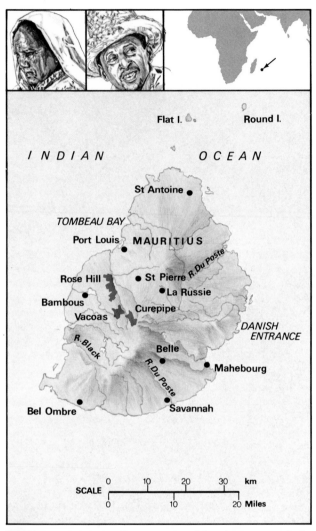

The people who live on Mauritius have two of the world's most vexatious problems. When you first see Mauritius, far out in the Indian Ocean, 500 miles east of Madagascar, the problems do not immediately strike the eye. Except in the east where it is desert, it is a lush green island, formerly volcanic, and surrounded by coral reefs everywhere but in the south, where the sea breaks directly on the coast. Fantastically shaped rocky peaks rise sharply from the fields of bright green sugar cane, planted where the land has been cleared of volcanic rock. Land is at a premium in Mauritius, for the islanders' greatest problem is overcrowding. And added to this, the huge population is not at peace with itself: it is divided over and over by racial, religious and social barriers which hamper any solution. Mauritius is a microcosm of the world's two most pressing social problems.

It is a semi-tropical, warm, humid island with dry desert in the west watered by only about 25 inches of annual rainfall and a lush central plateau where the rain-

The 'creoles' — descendants of
French settlers and African
slaves — form a quarter of the
island's dense population: this
young bride will add to it.

People of Mauritius

French settlers — who gave the *lingua franca* and the Roman Catholic faith to much of the island — still play a key part in politics and business.

fall may be as much as 200 inches. In the summer the island is hit by the south-east trade winds bringing heavy rain and sometimes, to the terror of all the islanders, cyclones which destroy property and plantations.

Sugar cane is the overstrained basis of the economy of the island, which has no natural resources to support the multi-ethnic society of 850,000 people who live jam-packed in an area of 720 square miles, just one tenth the size of New Jersey or Wales. The vast majority of this swelling population has to make its living in one way or another from this simple commodity of sugar. It does not do so as successfully as it needs to.

Yet just 400 years ago there was not one single human being, of any race, on Mauritius. When the Portuguese discovered this virgin island in the 16th century there were not even any mammals, except for vast, fruit-eating bats. There were birds, including some extraordinary large flightless ones, the most famous of which was the dodo – Mauritius has often been called Dodo Island after this bird. The Portuguese provisioned their ships, cut down trees and released pigs, goats, monkeys and, by mistake, rats, radically altering the island's ecology, but they never settled on the island. In 1598 the Dutch landed there, named the island after Prince Maurice of Nassau and during the 17th century twice tried to settle

Mauritius and exploit its ebony forests. They imported slaves from Madagascar and introduced sugar cane, tobacco, cotton, cattle and deer.

From its very beginning as an inhabited island, Mauritius was to be multi-ethnic. But the Dutch never built up a big enough labor force to make a successful colony and abandoned the island in 1710 leaving, perhaps, a few runaway slaves in the interior. In 1715 the French claimed the island, renamed it Ile de France and brought in colonists from the neighboring island of Bourbon (now Réunion), a French possession since 1654. They too imported slaves in large numbers from Africa and Madagascar – and established coffee, cotton, spice and sugar plantations. Sugar cane, which resisted damage by cyclones, was the most successful crop.

While Mahé de Labourdonnais was governor of the island (1735-1746) he improved the port and built forts, barracks, stores and ships. He backed up the Ile de France's reliance on African slaves by importing Indians from the French colonies in south India to work as artisans, messengers and servants. In 1746 he sailed in Mauritian-built ships with an army of slaves and colonists to India where he relieved Pondicherry and captured Madras from the British. The Ile de France developed as an important base for controlling shipping on the Indian

While Mauritians pull in the offshore fish, the big harbor at Port Louis has become a major base for deep sea trawlers.

(Bottom) Sugar is the only crop which successfully withstands the cyclones – and so cane cutting and refining has become a way of life to many.

trade routes. After successive attempts from 1748 to seize the island the British finally captured it with a force of 10,000 men and 60 vessels in 1810 and had their possession of the island confirmed by the Treaty of Paris in 1814.

The new British colony (which the British changed back from Ile de France to its earlier Dutch name of Mauritius) had a population of 78,000 – 63,000 of them slaves from East and West Africa and from negro Malagasy tribes, who had, through capture and sale in the slave markets – no respecters of family and cultural traditions – lost most of their original cultures and acquired a version of French culture which they molded and modified as their conditions permitted, creating notably the creole language, a simplified, lively form of French that has become the *lingua franca* of the island. The British also found 6,900 French who were mostly planters, merchants and civil servants. Under the Treaty of Capitulation, the French were permitted to retain their customs, language and religion, and to this day French culture, language and Roman Catholicism have remained prominent features of Mauritian life. Britons did not settle in Mauritius, and the agricultural estates, much commerce, and many government positions remained in French hands.

Between the French and the African slaves, about 10 per cent of the population was a class of free blacks and coloreds. The coloreds were children of the offspring of Frenchmen and African women, and were often freed by their fathers. Under the French *code noir* marriage between Europeans and slaves was forbidden. Free blacks and colored married among themselves, and their numbers increased. They became artisans and civil servants, and a few sat in the Colonial Assembly, which was set up at the time of the French Revolution.

Between 1835 and 1907 nearly 450,000 Indians were brought to Mauritius under various systems of indenture which bound them to work on the sugar estates for very low wages. Most of the Indians came from Bihar, the United Province (now Uttar Pradesh), Orissa and Bengal; others came from the Tamil and Telegu-speaking areas of south India, and a few came from the Marathi-speaking areas around Bombay. The vast majority of them were Hindus; some were Muslims, a few were Christians. They were of many castes although nearly all were poor. The immigrants were however able to indenture together and bring their wives and children. Thus though the conditions under which they served were harsh, the Indians did not suffer the disruption and fragmentation of their lives which was the fate of the African slaves. A final group of Indian immigrants were traders from Bombay and the Gujarati-speaking areas of west India. Most of these were Muslims, who became dealers in rice and cloth.

The Indian immigration radically changed the composition of the population. In 1835, there were only a handful of Indians; ten years later, one third of the

97

People of Mauritius

duced and by 1952 the malarial mosquito had been eradicated. In one year, the death rate fell by 32 per cent and at the same time, the birthrate rose. The population doubled between 1944 and 1972.

Of the two thirds Indian majority 51 per cent are Hindu and 16 per cent Muslim, and they are of five linguistic groups. The creoles of mixed African, Indian and/or European descent account for 28 per cent. They are nearly all Roman Catholics. Three per cent are Chinese, who speak two different dialects. An estimated two per cent are European, most of French ancestry.

The descendants of the immigrants into Mauritius have not amalgamated to become a homogeneous people. People align themselves against their neighbors on the grounds of religion, language and race. The word Mauritian itself when used on the island may mean, not as one might imagine any of the inhabitants of Mauritius, but only people of French descent or, in another context, creoles with light skin color. It rarely refers to Indians or Chinese. The word 'Indian' usually means Hindu rather than Muslim. Even the word Hindu usually means a northern rather than a southern Hindu. Different traditions are manifested in dress – the saris of Indian women, the Muslim fez, and the Chinese pajama – and in religious buildings – the domed mosque, the white northern Hindu temple and the polychromed southern Hindu one, the Roman Catholic church, the Chinese pagoda. They can be heard in the babel of the streets – Hindi, French, Gujarati, Urdu, English, Cantonese, Marathi, Hakka, Tamil, Telegu and most frequently, creole, the common language, the creation of the slaves. It is a diverse society. Mauritians of different ethnic backgrounds however do obviously affect each other and there is a constant interplay of forces now pushing the different groups together, now pulling them apart.

The very smallness of the island is a cohesive force. So is the excellent system of roads and public transport. Although Mauritius is an agricultural country and most people live in the countryside, the remotest villager can with relative ease reach the towns which stretch from Port Louis, the capital and chief port on the south-east coast, up to Curepipe, high on the central plateau. The 44 per cent of the population who live in the towns are not segregated into ethnic ghettos. Most villages contain people of more than one ethnic group. In their daily lives the vast majority of Mauritians have contact with people of different ethnic groups than their own.

And although most sugar estate owners are Franco-Mauritians, most retail shopkeepers are Chinese, most agricultural laborers are Indians, and most artisans are creoles, there are Indian sugar estate owners, Muslim shopkeepers, creole laborers and Chinese artisans. It is certainly an oversimplification to assume that each ethnic group is confined to a particular occupation. And in some occupations – notably the civil service – people of all ethnic groups fiercely compete. The result is that within

population was Indian, and 16 years after that, in 1861, two thirds of the population was Indian, a proportion maintained to the present.

The Chinese, the final element in the Mauritian ethnic kaleidoscope, came mostly from south China, and their numbers greatly increased after World War II. They became shopkeepers and merchants, and many intermarried with the creole population. Some speak Cantonese; others Hakka and while about half the Chinese population adhere to traditional forms of Chinese religion, the other half are Christian.

Although the population of Mauritius grew with the European, African and then Indian immigrations in the 18th and 19th centuries, during all this period, there was little natural population increase. The population was continually decimated by plagues and epidemics. Infant mortality was high. Malaria, which reached Mauritius in 1865, was the great killer. In April 1867 one twelfth of the population of Port Louis died: the death rate for the island in that year reached 247 per 1,000. Population growth was effectively controlled by malaria. But in 1948 a massive campaign of spraying with DDT was intro-

Infant mortality — especially from malaria — has been sharply reduced. One result has been the doubling of the population between 1944 and 1972.

Curbing over-population is critical: a member of the Mauritian Family Planning Association introduces women to methods of birth control.

each ethnic group there is a considerable range of income and an upper, middle and lower class. Not that this is necessarily a unifying factor in this already fiercely divided society. Ethnic divisiveness can give way to class divisiveness.

Nevertheless there are possibilities for economic interests to cut across ethnic boundaries, and the Muslim or Chinese wholesaler, for example, may find he has more in common with the Franco-Mauritian estate-owner than with the poorest members of his own race or faith. The Indian field laborer and the creole dock worker discover common economic and political interests. The new identities create new problems. A set of loyalties rooted in a man's ethnicity, religion and language, can conflict with another set attached to his occupation, economic class and his way of life.

Until 1948 only males who owned substantial property or who had a monthly income of at least 50 rupees could vote and until then there was little political outlet for the expressions of conflict. The vast majority of Indians and a large proportion of creoles were effectively disfranchised. Power rested with a small oligarchy of Franco-Mauritian planters and a few creoles under the not-always-very-watchful eye of the British Colonial Office. It was the educated creoles who first protested against this system, and in 1936 founded the Mauritius Labor Party under Dr Maurice Curé who developed a growing following of Indian laborers and small planters. The move towards a more representative government was accelerated by labor unrest in 1937 and again in 1943. In 1948 when the right to vote was extended to both sexes, with a simple literacy or property-holding qualification, the electorate increased from about 12,000 in 1946 to nearly 72,000 in the 1948 elections. For the first time the majority element of the population was able to elect a majority to the Legislative Council and control passed from Franco-Mauritians and creoles to the Indians. Ethnicity had entered politics.

The situation posed a dilemma for the creoles. Some felt their economic and class interests were with the Indians in the Labor Party. Others felt their best interests lay with the Franco-Mauritians with whom they shared a common French culture and Roman Catholicism. Franco-Mauritian papers published articles about the Hindu menace. Muslims began to feel threatened as a minority and started to organize their own party. Soon a Hindu party was formed. And although the Labor Party remained multi-ethnic — with Hindu, Muslim and creole members — the specter of communal conflict emerged. Presented with the dilemma that majority rule threatened minority interests, a British Commission visited the island in 1957 and divided it into 40 single-member constituencies so that each ethnic category would be represented in the Legislature in proportion roughly equivalent to their number in the total population. This solution turned out to be impracticable because unfortunately the Muslims, 99

Mosques, churches, temples and pagodas abound to accommodate the different faiths. This Indian woman prays in a Hindu place of worship.

for example, live so widely dispersed throughout the island that there was no way of forming geographical constituencies which would give them representation corresponding to their numbers. Moreover this system tended to destroy the political parties. In the tiny constituencies small parties and independent candidates emerged who appealed to even more narrowly divisive local issues, to some local form of ethnic affiliation such as Tamil-speakers or to a particular caste origin. Meanwhile, the island was moving steadily towards independence, which made the struggle for power more intense.

In 1966 another new constitution was produced by which there were to be 70 members of the Legislature. The island was divided into 20 three-member constituencies, so that each voter could vote for three candidates. It was hoped that even if a voter voted on ethnic, linguistic or religious lines for his first and second choice, he would vote on party lines for his third.

Elections under this constitution led to independence in March 1968. There have been no elections since, and members of the opposition parties have been taken into the Labor Party government, headed by an Indian (Sir Seewoosagur Ramgoolam).

Seats in the Legislature have eased but not solved Mauritius' apparently intractable problems. With no natural resources Mauritius' greatest asset, a large literate, low paid labor force, is also her greatest liability. The swelling population ominously dumps ever-increasing numbers of young people on the tiny job market. There were three means, all desperately needed and all beset by obstacles, by which Mauritius could try to solve her population problem: emigration, increased productivity and birth control.

There have been many schemes, all of which have foundered, for Mauritians to emigrate to Borneo, East Africa, Madagascar, British Honduras. There has even been a proposal that Mauritius should integrate with Britain. Each of these countries was either unwilling to accept an influx of Mauritians or demanded much higher subsidies than the Mauritian government could afford. Emigration prospects for most Mauritians remain bleak.

The government has tried to exploit its vast pool of workless labor and step up productivity by creating favorable conditions for foreign manufacturers to set up factories on the island. But Mauritius is so far away from world markets that manufacturers would lose in increased transport costs what they could save in cheap labor. Schemes are nevertheless under way for the manufacture of jewels for watches, and of wigs – lightweight and therefore cheaply transportable products which require a high input of labor. Mauritius still has to import most of its food but the government is trying to encourage Mauritians to take marginal sugar cane lands out of production and to grow more food crops. They do export cash crops such as tea, ginger, tropical fruit and flowers, and there are attempts to increase milk and

Hindus hold fire-walking
rites to ensure a bountiful
sugar harvest. Children are
carried across the hot coals,
but the parents walk on them.

Piercing of the lips with
miniature silver swords is
practised as a tribute to
village deities who will
in turn give good health.

meat production and to develop deep sea fishing. Also Mauritius is developing facilities for tourists. Nevertheless Mauritius' economic opportunities are extremely limited. Its population is not.

It was not only because of the general world attitude towards birth control, which shifted radically in the 1960s, that little was done to enable Mauritians to practise birth control until the late 1960s. It was partly because of the fear of communal conflict which advocating birth control might engender. The Roman Catholic Church and many Muslims on the island were adamantly opposed to birth control. Hindus, who frequently cited the Indian government's advocacy of birth control, were much less opposed. Local politicians struggling for power exploited the issue. Although a voluntary family planning association was founded in 1957, during crucial years of population growth, little was accomplished. Official government support and overseas aid was not forthcoming until the late 1960s. The birth rate has recently shown a decline from over three per cent per annum in 1968 to just over two per cent in 1971. It remains unclear, however, whether individual Mauritians see their life chances improved by having fewer children. What is clear is that the rest of the world will have to rescue this island people from the consequences of their overbreeding.

101

(Over page) At a Hindu
cremation, friends and
relatives pay the deceased
their final respects just
before the pyre is lit.

Chokwe
Angola

The Chokwe's famous and
unusual masks are made to
frighten away evil spirits
from important ceremonies,
especially circumcision rites.

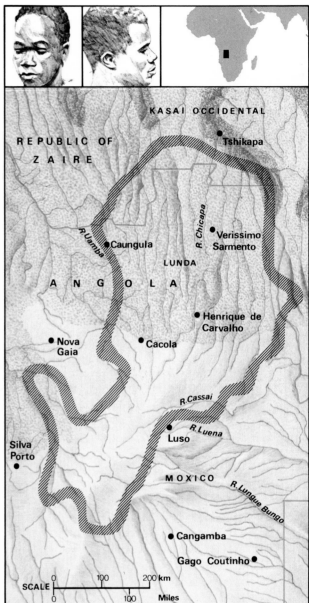

In the years since the Chokwe people were first invaded by Lunda nobles and tribesmen from the north, and then later by Portuguese colonists, many have migrated away from their original homeland in the desolate scrub and savanna of north-east Angola. Today there are Chokwe settlements in Zaïre and Zambia as well; and there may be at least 600,000 Chokwe people. In their village settlements the Chokwe live by farming – the cultivation of their staple crop, manioc (cassava) is mainly in the hands of women – and hunting; but above all, the Chokwe are craftsmen. It is this that marks them out among the people of this region; this and the brotherhoods and ceremonies which hold their people together.

The Chokwe hunters hunt with traps or by driving the 105

Chokwe Angola

animals before them as they burn the dry grasses of the
savanna. Professional hunters, however, belong to a
special brotherhood. To join this brotherhood a man has
to be singled out by a spirit who will, before the initiation
ceremony, take possession of him. The father of the
brotherhood makes charms for all the members to help
them in the hunt. And whenever a hunter makes a kill
on his own, he keeps a rear paw of the animal to present
to his chief. The brotherhood, the spirit, the initiation
ceremony and even the chief are all fundamental to the
Chokwe way of life.

The Chokwe chief is a sacred person who is protected
by the ancestors. He is the arbiter of all legal and secular
conflicts and a power for fertility. His symbol of authority
is the *lukano* bracelet which used to be made of male

This realistic carving of a
circumcision has the vigor and
liveliness that makes Chokwe
sculpture some of the best and
most famous in Africa.

Last year's initiates will dance
to encourage the boys whose
turn it is now. No women
or uncircumcised people are
allowed to watch the rites.

genitalia of enemies. Around the chief gathered the court: the nobles who acted as judges, lawyers, doctors and masters of the cult of ancestors. In the past the most important chiefs also had a warlord and an élite corps of ten or twenty specially chosen young warriors. The chief's sister acts as his councillor and from her sons – for the Chokwe's is a matrilineal society – the next chief is chosen. The chief's mother, sister of the preceding chief, was traditionally also highly regarded and exerted much influence on her son.

In Chokwe village life, the sooth-sayer is second only in the hierarchy to the nobles. He is called in on all important occasions – to detect evil and to divine the hidden wishes of the spirits. At the time of a man's death or illness, a woman's barrenness, an unsuccessful hunt, or even the theft of an object, the soothsayer will bring his basket containing 60 or more symbolic objects – figurines, bird-beaks, boots, nails, stones and fruits, all bearing markings in white and red clay – which he then shakes. The white clay marks symbolize good, the red markings symbolize evil, and the soothsayer's interpretation of the occasion will depend on the manner in which these objects fall as he shakes them, and onto which color markings. Should a figurine representing an ancestor fall on a red marking, it means that illness has been invoked by the anger of that spirit. Perhaps the spirit has been neglected, or even forgotten. To cure the illness it is then necessary to carve a figurine of the spirit and honor it with sacrifices of animal blood.

The Chokwe believe in a supreme being, Nzambi, but do not support their belief by any organized religion, except through the ancestor spirits or *mahamba* who mediate between Nzambi and men. These spirits are represented by trees and symbolized by wooden or earthenware figurines to which the Chokwe regularly make sacrifices and gifts. The family *mahamba* are housed in an enclosure behind every family hut. An enclosure behind the chief's hut houses the most important *mahamba,* the protectors of his family and the whole community. The Chokwe also respect other spirits: the *akishi,* symbolized by resin and wooden masks, and the evil *wanga* which witchdoctors imprison in containers with poisonous substances.

At the time of puberty, Chokwe girls and boys undergo the *mukanda* initiation ceremony which introduces them to the secrets of adult life. The boys are circumcised, secluded for a time from contact with women, and then given a period of learning. They learn about the *mukanda* masks which are worn by the dancers during the ceremony; they learn about the other masked figures which appear at festival time; they learn that these are not incarnated spirits – as uninitiated men and terrified women believe they are – but in fact their fathers and uncles and cousins dressed up. During this time, the initiates also learn about dancing and music and carving. Every one of these initiates considered himself a potential expert, for the Chokwe artists are respected men. Although the Chokwe distinguish between only two types of artist – the *songi* woodcarver and the *fuli* blacksmith – objects produced in clay, bark cloth, leather, fibers and reeds are also thought aesthetic.

It is the masked dancers who conduct the *mukanda* ceremonies that are the prime subjects of Chokwe art. There are about thirty stock characters, mostly made in bark cloth or carved from wood. The *mukanda* is a ceremony by which religious beliefs and art are transmitted to the next generation in a secret and dramatic manner. The new generation learn how to make these *mukanda* masks, the *mahamba* figurines for their shrines, and the charms, the *jinga,* which are used in hunting, love and magic fertility rites. Carvers and basketmakers can become famous for their works; often they are considered professional despite their attachment to a little farming with which to supplement their income. Many of the Chokwe chiefs still own carved thrones which are among the largest and most fantastic ever created by African artists. On the sides of these thrones are carved scenes depicting *mukanda* circumcision ceremonies, women at their work pounding a mortar, rows of dancers in grass skirts, soldiers with rifles, abstract animals and even erotic subjects. The thrones are the most spectacular form of Chokwe art and as with so many other objects, they are elaborate and carved far beyond the needs of their function. From the elaborate chiefly objects like scepters, pipes and snuff-boxes, to the carved domestic objects like walking sticks, clubs and drums, the Chokwe preserve a refined artistic tradition. Perhaps this has happened because of the importance of these objects in the *mukanda* ceremony, which itself preserves the identity of the people.

Herero
South-west Africa

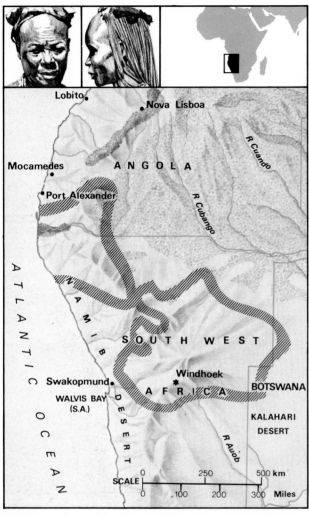

H erero legend has it that long ago a group of people, led by Kathu and his brother Nangombe, left the country of many fountains and wandered south and westwards in search of a new dwelling place. After enduring many hardships they came to a big tree called the omumborombonga tree where the two brothers decided to part. Kathu gathered his followers and wandered until he came to what is now known as Namibia or South-west Africa where he and his people settled. The 'country of many fountains', their country of origin, is supposed to be the area west of Lake Tanganyika. 'Long ago' is most likely the middle of the 15th century. Certainly the Herero reached their destination in Namibia in the middle of the 16th century. Three centuries later, when the Germans arrived in their homeland, about 80,000 Herero lived in an area which stretched from Kaokveldt in the north-west, southwards and eastwards almost to Windhoek.

Since the Herero were, as they still are, cattle-raisers, their most needed resource was grazing-land. The Germans, who were under the impression that a tribe

Herero women are the social
equals of men and it is the
mother and her clan who
decide on the size of a
boy's cattle inheritance.

Herero South-west Africa

Many Herero are Christians today. For weddings they have adopted Victorian dress which they wear with a cloth 'duk' around their heads.

For the first six months after marriage a Herero girl must keep her face covered continually by a veil of beads.

necessarily had to have exactly bounded tribal land, were puzzled and confused to find that the Herero did not draw exact boundaries to their land. It was not in the Herero tradition to do so, although in practice the presence of ethnic groups as neighbors effectively acted as boundaries. In the south, for instance, lived the Nama who had reacted to European expansion by migrating from the Cape. Before the Germans arrived the two groups had been sufficiently boundary-conscious to have waged disputes that degenerated into sporadic warfare.

The Germans launched their colony of South-west Africa when they hoisted their flag in Luderitz Bay in 1884, and immediately tried to establish a well-oiled political machinery by winning over indigenous chiefs. They would manipulate political differences between them and suddenly punish leaders who did not comply with their wishes. These policies had manifestly failed after a few years when the indigenous ethnic groups rose against them. The two rebellions that are best remembered were those of the Nama and the Herero.

The Herero struck suddenly and with unexpected force in January 1904. More than a hundred German men, soldiers and settlers were surprised and killed. The railway between Windhoek and Swakopmund was destroyed in several places and telegraph communications were broken. The Germans were taken unawares and the Herero seized and kept control in their own area for seven months. But in August when most of the Herero forces gathered together around the water holes by Hamakari river with their women, children and cattle, the Germans – led by General von Trotha who had earlier crushed the Hehe uprising in Tanganyika – surrounded them. They waged a ruthless battle intended to take the entire Herero forces prisoner. The battle was long drawn-out and the Herero finished by fleeing eastwards. The Germans pursued them into the desert area of Omaheke where many Herero died of thirst, heat and exhaustion. Some of them, with their chief Samuel Maharero, fled to what is now Botswana where their descendants still live.

In Namibia von Trotha adopted a policy of exterminating all the remaining Herero. 'Inside German territory,' he declared, 'every Herero tribesman, armed or unarmed, with or without cattle, will be shot. No women and children will be allowed in the territory: they will be driven back to their people or fired on. These are the last words to the Herero nation from me, the great General of the mighty German Emperor.'

By the time von Trotha was recalled (for political reasons in 1905) 80 per cent of the Herero had been killed; only 12,000 arrived in the special camps set up by the new governor and some of the missions.

The war and the subsequent relentless extermination of this vast number of their forbears is still vivid in the Herero mind. The terrible story is passed down from old to young and has contributed to a feeling of Herero

111

The sea shell round this young bride's neck is a highly prized heirloom. Very large or unusual shells may be traded for a cow.

On the graves of their dead Herero pile up the horns of cattle that have been slaughtered in honor of the deceased.

identity and to a pride in their culture and history. Indeed so strong is the Herero identity, to others as well as to themselves, that Herero are often referred to, mistakenly, as 'the Herero nation', implying that they are a nation within a nation. This is misleading. For although the Herero call themselves Herero, speak their own language and retain their own political organization, their primary identification is with Namibia, governed virtually as a province of South Africa since 1949. The Herero identity rests in a sense of a common heritage, a common ancestry by which most Herero feel that they are related to other Herero, and a feeling that because of this they owe each other loyalty.

The traditional forms of Herero life are based on cattle farming, much as they are among other cattle-raising people in central and east Africa and the Sudan. Cattle are capital and prestige; through cattle marriage alliances are established; cattle are used as compensation and are admired, loved and praised in songs. When after the Herero-German war the Germans forbade the Herero to own cattle, they destroyed the economic structure of Herero life. It is a grave challenge to the culture of the Herero that today they live in reserves too limited in grazing resources for extensive cattle-raising. There are many Herero who live in urban areas, often as traders, shopkeepers and professional people – within the limits set by the South African administration. The cattle-population is low and, except as food and as a social medium in exchanges, is now of little economic value.

When the South African government revealed its plans to move the Herero from their present reserve further north and west to the Rietfontein Block, which would be unsuitable for cattle-raising, the Herero protested so strongly against this attempt to force them to move that the government gave way. In Namibia as in many parts of Africa, land is not owned in the same way as in Europe. Land is for use, not for ownership. Thus it is the right to use and not the title to ownership of a piece of land that is inherited. This may seem confusing to an outsider, and has frequently been a source of conflict.

From the day he is born a Herero child belongs to three different groups. The most important of these is his mother's *eanda* – often translated as clan. The vital part a child's mother plays in his life derives from something more than her role in rearing him. She, and her clan, determine his inheritance of cattle. There are then his father's *oruzo,* or paternal clan, which is mainly a ritual group, and a third group, in whose name the child is praised, his father's father's *oruzo*. Although it happens that his father's *oruzo* and his father's father's *oruzo* bear the same name, a child's three groups should ideally have three different names. In some instances even a child's *eanda* may have not only the same name as his father's *oruzo,* but also that of his father's father. In such cases a child is not considered properly bred, and is in fact usually a bastard.

112

Small shells are made into intricate head-dresses which are worn by men as well as women, although the women's are usually more elaborate.

The *eanda,* the maternal clan, is the main property-holding group and cattle is the most important property inherited through the mother – apart from membership of a group. The Herero believe that whereas a child is the child of his father he *is* his mother and is therefore closer to her. If a couple wants to part, it is not easy for the father to claim his child. The mother's family will ask 'Who carried the child for nine months? Who built the house in which the child grew up? And who was it who reared the child?' To each question the answer is 'his mother'.

The importance of the child's relation with his mother is consolidated by the fact that a child is placed in his mother's brother's kinship group. Cattle may no longer be the basis of the Herero economy but they remain at the basis of Herero family and social life. At his name-giving ceremony – traditionally by the Herero holy fire – a child is usually given his first head of cattle and he receives more cattle as he grows up. A boy's cattle will eventually constitute his bridewealth when he marries.

Six to eight year old boys are traditionally secluded together for six to eight weeks when they undergo the circumcision ceremony. As they grow up they regard themselves as 'coevals', members of a special kind of brotherhood, who can call upon each other as of right in times of stress and difficulty, and can count on each other's full support in all circumstances. A Herero cannot refuse a coeval anything. He will tell you that if his coeval comes to his house and asks him to give him a goat or a piece of furniture, he has to give it to him. Although the full circumcision ceremony is no longer universal the circumcision operation itself prevails and so do the bonds of brotherhood of coevals.

Ever since the Herero-Nama war in the latter part of the 19th century, when various chiefs co-operated to stand more strongly against the Nama Maharero of Okahandja, the Herero have been united under one paramount chief. Before, they were organized in smaller groups each headed by a chief and his council. The new arrangement suited not only the Herero, but also the European traders and missionaries, because it enabled them to obtain guarantees of free movement within Herero territory. The arrangement became permanent and consolidated the Herero chiefly traditions. The present paramount chief has his center in Okahandja, the site of the graves of chief Tjamuha Maharero, of his son Samuel Maharero, and of Hosea Kutako, who died aged almost 100 in July 1970.

After the German-Herero war, when their chief Samuel Maharero was forced to flee to Botswana (then Bechuanaland), the Herero still in Namibia chose no new chief to replace him. He was their chief until 1923 when he died—not as he had always wanted, in Namibia. He did not live to see his own return, but his body was taken back and buried in Okahandja on 25th August 1923 – ever since the date and the place of the annual Otjiserandu

memorial ceremony which commemorates the Herero war against the Germans. To this Otjiserandu ceremony the men come dressed in their old, often German, uniforms and perform a military parade alongside the graves of their former chiefs. 'Otjiserandu' means red, a special color which stands today for 'hereroism'. It is conspicuous on the flag of the Otjiserandu, and in the dresses worn by the women at the ceremony. Herero women wear Victorian-style clothes. With a long dress with a wide, stiff skirt and a narrow bodice they wear a 'duk', a cloth wrapped around their heads. These clothes are of any color except during the Otjiserandu ceremony when both the 'duk' and the skirt are bright red with a black bodice. The Otjiserandu (or red) was originally associated with the holy fire.

The Herero believe in an omnipresent and omnipotent Ndjambi Karunga, giver of life and love. But most of their religious activity centers on their ancestors and on the holy fire. Their ancestors were ultimately descended from Mukuru, the old one, who came from the omumborombonga tree of the myth of origin. *Mukuru* also means 'ancestor' generally, thus each family has its own *mukuru* or founder of the family group.

The head of a homestead or family group has certain religious duties inherited through his father through his membership of the *oruzo*. Of these the most important was his sacred duty, when a chief or head of a family died, to kindle the holy fire. The holy fire is kindled with two sticks, one regarded as a 'male' stick called *ondume* (derived from the verb *okuruma* meaning 'to live together as man and wife'); the other regarded as a 'female' stick and called *otjitja* derived from the verb *okuja,* 'to come'. The holy fire symbolizes fertility, prosperity and a good relationship with the ancestors, and the ritual with the sticks confirms the ideal way in which the family should live and prosper, with the woman coming to live with her husband, and the husband treating her in the traditional, proper way.

The way in which the holy fire is looked after reflects the equal social importance of men and women in Herero society. While it is the duty of the male head of the family to kindle the fire, it is his eldest daughter's duty to keep it alive. When the girl, called *omurangere,* 'a person having ritual duties', married and moved out of her father's home, she would move out of the ritual sphere of her father's home into that of her husband. Her ritual duties would be undertaken by someone else, probably her mother.

As most Herero today are Christians the old ritual customs no longer play quite the same role. But the holy fire has not been extinguished. It is still a symbol of fertility, health and prosperity in a family, and is usually kept by one of the elders. The red fire is an essential element in the Herero identity, a symbol of the continuation of Herero life which so many forces have tried to exterminate.

113

Bushmen
Southern Africa

'Old Abraham', chief of
Africa's oldest race, died
recently aged 107.
The horn on his cap is
a symbol of high status.

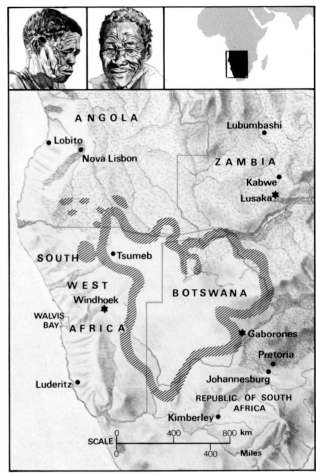

When the Bushmen find a tree in the desert which is heavy with fruit, they stop their wanderings for a time, and build temporary huts in the sandy scrub. Groups of thirty or forty people camp like this among grey-green stunted trees, standing and sitting companionably in small family groups. There has to be water within reach. The men are thin and the women lumpily fat with wide brows, slanting eyes, high cheek bones and high breasts, all brown-skinned and almost naked except for soft leather aprons. The women carry their babies slung round their hips, and everybody looks hungry; the expressions on the flat mongoloid faces are reserved even when they smile. In some groups the people have filed or broken their front teeth into jagged points, and the women scar their skin into careful patterns, which their husbands like to touch more than smooth skin. They wear a lot of jewelry and ostrich eggshell beads, and the women are particularly careful about their appearance. Bushmen are relatively pale for an African people, usually about five feet tall, with hair growing in peppercorn tufts. They are extremely hardy: the fat on the women's buttocks and thighs is a reserve for lean times, rather like a camel's hump.

Bushmen southern Africa

The Bushmen have only recently abandoned their most highly developed and characteristic art, painting and engraving on rocks and cave walls.

If hunting has been successful there will be a feast under the fruit tree, with porcupine and roasted caterpillar perhaps. Everybody shares, except children under three who still drink their mother's milk, and the Bushmen eat every part of the animals they have caught.

The Bushmen are now refugees, displaced persons, the cornered relics of a people who once occupied vast areas of Africa as well as the south. In Tanzania, in Ethiopia and Uganda and in southern Sudan, their beautiful rock paintings have been discovered, and some of their artifacts such as the perforated stone spheres which they still use to weigh down their digging sticks. And throughout southern Africa there are abundant signs of their earlier presence: those rock paintings again, place-names which derive from their languages, and their own very distinctive skeletal remains. No one is sure where they came from and their mongol strain is a mystery.

They have long been on the retreat. Between the 12th and 15th centuries AD people of the Bushman type having by then been driven down into what we now call South Africa were penetrated by two successive waves of Bantu people, whose more developed cultures included agriculture and the herding of cattle. Some Bushmen adopted these practices and were later known as Hottentots. The term Bushman was devised by the early European settlers to apply to the people who, unlike the Hottentot pasturalists, were nomads. Under pressure from black men from the north and white men from the south they had retreated into the arid loess of the Kalahari Desert where the advantage lay with those who still lived the old hunting and gathering way of life.

Today it is easy to confuse Bushmen with Hottentots and Bantu people, with whom they have intermarried. Both Hottentots and Bushmen speak similar, related 'click' languages. And many Bushmen have lost their distinctive way of life. Bushmen women, for example, are keen to scrape up their hair in Bantu-looking fuzz. Some Bushmen have settled and started to work for wages on European farms. Others have formed close relationships with neighboring African peoples – especially the Tswana – and work for them as hunters, laborers and cattlemen in return for food, livestock, clothing and tobacco. But in and near the Kalahari Desert they remain a nomad people, divisible into several distinct linguistic groups, and living in small bands of 25 to 60 people by the ancient economy of hunting and gathering with no agriculture and no domestic animals. Their Kalahari Desert retreat is, fortunately for the Bushmen, not fully a desert. It has an annual rainfall which varies from 20 inches in the north-east to 5 inches in the south-west. During the rainy season not only does grass grow everywhere, so does other vegetation varying from thick forest to low thorn scrub. It also has a population of large game animals.

Each hunting band is divided into families, made up of a man, his wife or (occasionally) wives, and their dependent children. Among certain tribes a young man who

116

Surviving from pre-literal times, rock art is important as a source of information about the life of early man in Europe and throughout Africa.

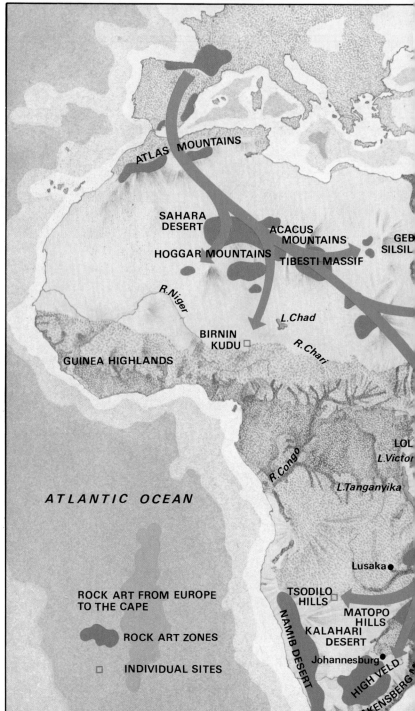

ATLAS MOUNTAINS

SAHARA DESERT

ACACUS MOUNTAINS

HOGGAR MOUNTAINS

TIBESTI MASSIF

GEB SILSIL

R.Niger

L.Chad

BIRNIN KUDU

R.Chari

GUINEA HIGHLANDS

R.Congo

LOL

L.Victor

L.Tanganyika

ATLANTIC OCEAN

Lusaka

ROCK ART FROM EUROPE TO THE CAPE

TSODILO HILLS

MATOPO HILLS

ROCK ART ZONES

NAMIB DESERT

KALAHARI DESERT

Johannesburg

INDIVIDUAL SITES

HIGH VELD

DRAKENSBERG

wants to get married has to do long service for his bride's parents: he may have to live with them if they belong to another band and in a limited and temporary way extended families come into being. There is a natural but informal tendency for the older men and the more experienced and skilful hunters to direct the band's activities. And in some tribes there are hereditary chiefs with authority over hunting and ritual and the vital question of the supply and use of water. But within each band there is no real government, no formal authority, no system of law and punishment. The individual redresses his grievances privately, if at all, and only in extreme cases by violence, which is feared and disliked by these notably peaceful, gentle people. If a Bushman is persistently anti-social his band may ostracize or even expel him.

Within each tribe the various bands live together as equals. Each has hunting and gathering rights over its own territory and within its own boundaries. And although the Kalahari landscape may seem featureless, Bushmen know and respect these boundaries precisely. But between different bands there are many contacts of trade and marriage and mere sociability. Individuals often move from one band to another, and any single band will therefore vary widely in its size and membership over quite a short period. In the dry season it may break up altogether, and its members may go off and live temporarily as single-family units.

Most Bushmen are monogamous but if a man is a skilful enough hunter to provide meat for more than one family, he can take a second wife or, very exceptionally, more. A second wife will usually be the sister of the first, on the assumption that this will minimize the quarreling and jealousy to which polygamous households are often prone. Adultery is rare, but divorce is possible if either party desires it. After either divorce or death they usually re-marry and the second spouse is often the brother or sister of the first.

Among the Kung Bushmen a girl is married in early childhood to an adolescent boy, who must previously have proved his manhood by killing a large game animal and by undergoing a ceremonial initiation. His young bride will commonly come from another band, since most members of the same band are related – either by blood or by special convention which gives people a bond of kinship although they are related neither by blood nor by marriage. The groom usually joins the girl's band and works for her parents for a number of years, perhaps remaining with them permanently or perhaps returning to his own in due course.

Since Bushmen have no cattle, there is no milk for children. Each child is therefore breastfed until the age of two or three years, which means that other children born during that time cannot be fed at all. According to some accounts, such babies are killed at birth, before they can 'cry in the mother's heart', as the Bushmen put

117

A hunting band prepares to leave the shade of a hardy tree in search of food and water. The adults wear cloaks of sewn animal skins.

This woman, like all her people, sleeps comfortably in a sheltered hollow scraped out of the loess, a skin cloak her only cover.

it. Perhaps for this reason families stay small and the population is stable at the level of self-support in the harsh and limited environment of the Kalahari. There is another possible reason why families are small. According to the Bushmen themselves their women are naturally sterile during the dry season.

According to some accounts, Bushmen will build a shelter around an aging couple as some protection against wild animals, leave them there with as much food and water as can be spared, and then move on, weeping bitterly. The old people's solitude will not last long. Probably before their food and water are exhausted, a leopard or a hyena will break in and eat them.

The Bushmen normally bury their dead. They lay the corpse on its side in a foetal position with the knees drawn up. They bury the dead man's possessions with him and avoid the spot for a year or two afterwards. Bushmen do not make a cult of their ancestors, as most Bantu do, but they believe in the importance and continuing presence of the spirits of their dead. They are secretive about their other religious beliefs, and confine the knowledge of the full mysteries to mature and initiated males. Among the Kung and the Gwi and possibly among other Bushmen there are two supernatural beings: one is the creator of this world and of life, while the other – a less powerful deity – is responsible for sickness and death.

Bushmen live by set patterns of social behavior. A Kung must be reserved and respectful towards the people who, by blood, marriage, or by a special convention, are placed in certain defined relationships with himself. But towards other people, differently related to him, he can joke freely, as between one equal and another. The system is extremely complicated but clear-cut, and it also governs the choice of a bride. Not only is actual incest forbidden. So is the strictly technical incest involved if a man marries a girl actually unrelated to him, but having the conventional title of his 'mother' or 'sister'. Personal names in use among the Kung are few, so that different individuals often bear the same name, and are then believed to stand in a special close relationship and even to share the same identity to some degree. This social system which seems complicated is fully understood and completely workable; it means that every Kung knows exactly where he stands in relation to every other man – even to a stranger from a remote band – and how he should behave towards him. It is a system which makes for psychological security and therefore for peace.

By contrast, the physical and technical arrangements of Bushmen life are visibly simple. Their houses are crude structures for temporary occupation, built of branches roofed with grass, and normally on a semi-circular ground plan, and semi-circular in profile. The women build these houses, one for each family, each one against a supporting tree and near a waterhole wherever possible. Inside the earth floor may be scooped out here and there

to accommodate the sleepers' hip-bones. Strips of venison may hang drying from the roof, but there is little ornament.

Their chief weapon is the bow and arrow tipped with poison obtained from snakes, plants or insects. They also hunt with spears, throwing-sticks, traps, snares, and sometimes they dig carefully disguised pitfalls. The women, armed with a digging stick sometimes weighted with a perforated stone, gather roots and other vegetable food. Their most valued possession is usually a large pestle and mortar, carved out of ironwood and used to pound nuts and seeds, and to make meat easier for the oldest and youngest to chew. To kindle fire they spin a stick against a piece of soft wood.

The Bushmen have little sense of private property. When a large animal is killed, they share out its meat as a matter of course between all the members of the band. But they also kill smaller animals for food, and not strictly by hunting techniques. They often extract spring-hares, porcupines, badgers, ground squirrels and other burrowing animals from their holes by the use of long hooked sticks, and the finder will usually reserve these for his own family.

The men wear a triangular loin-cloth and the women a small apron before and behind, these garments being of dressed skins. Both sexes also wear cloaks of sewn leather. They take trouble with their personal adornment. Women and children and the younger men wear beads made from fragments of ostrich eggshell. Some tribes paint their faces in black and red, and ritually scar and ornamentally tattoo themselves.

Living in such an arid region, the Bushmen are dependent upon what water is available. But they can find it where the unpractised eye would never suspect – a few feet below the surface of completely dry ground; and they suck it up through long tubes and transfer it to containers of ostrich eggshells, which they carry on the march and sometimes bury as an emergency reserve.

To a Bushman, this girl is a
real beauty. The fat on her
buttocks and thighs acts as
a food reserve, making her
a tough and hardy wife.

The ostrich egg carried by
this young girl is used as a
water container to be taken
on the march or buried as an
emergency water supply.

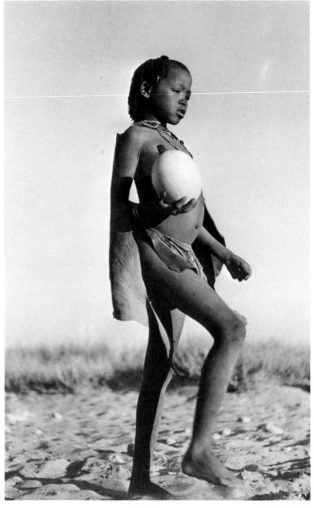

Children listen spellbound
to tales of ancient hunts.
Their hair curls in tight
'peppercorns' and some wear
beads made of ostrich eggshell.

These girls may already be married to boys little older than themselves who will have proved their manhood by killing a large game animal.

(Bottom) Each woman builds a temporary hut for her family of branches roofed with grass, wherever possible close to a waterhole.

In the night-long fire dance the medicine man finally works himself into a trance. Thus endowed with magical powers, he exorcises evil.

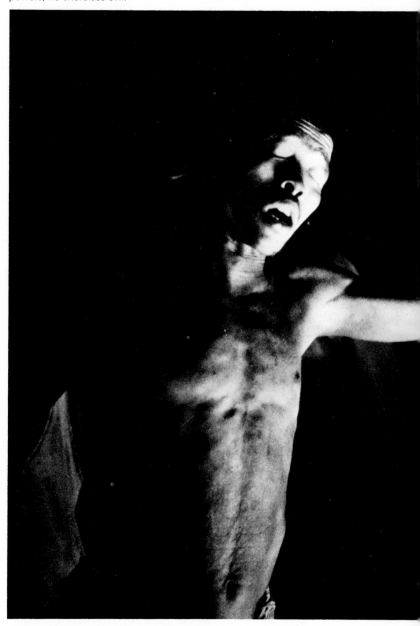

During the hot dry season, the Kalahari melon is a useful source of moisture as well as food.

The Bushmen enjoy art and are particularly fond of music, singing, and dancing. Their chief musical instrument is a kind of bow held against the mouth: the string is struck repeatedly, and the pitch of the resulting note is modified by the size of the oral cavity, rather on the principle of the Jew's harp. They also use a kind of four-stringed lyre, but – surprisingly in a people with such a sense of rhythm – they have no drums.

They often dance both for fun and for ritual. The fire-dance and the eland-dance are spectacular. Good Bushmen dancers must be excellent mimics and they can look startlingly like the animals and people they imitate.

When the moon is full, they often have a purification dance. A lone tree, sharp and black in the light of the night, is perhaps the landmark where they gather. All around stretches the loess of the Kalahari Desert. The women sit round a large fire, their babies asleep on their backs, and they start to sing medicine songs and clap their hands to a sharp staccato rhythm as the counterpoint to the surging lilt of their voices. The only musical instrument for the purification dance is the rattle made from cocoons dried and strung together with tiny pieces of ostrich eggshell inside.

One behind the other, with these rattles tied to their

Bushmen are talented mimics who accurately reproduce the appearance and sounds of the animals they hunt in their dances.

(Bottom) 'Dead' dancers are symbolically resurrected to the accompaniment of clapping. Surprisingly, Bushmen have no drums.

ankles, they slowly circle round and behind the backs of the women. Their short shuffling steps stir up clouds of dust from the dry desert sand. Now and then the men let out a series of throaty moans in harmony with the women. All the while their ankle-rattlers clatter.

The dance gradually speeds up; the singing gets louder, the atmosphere more intense. Then the medicine man, who has been leading the dancing men, suddenly leaps into the inner circle of women and dances round in a frenzy, shrieking and flinging his arms into the air. As he draws nearer and nearer to the flames the women try to hold him back, but he breaks loose, flings himself forward, and is immersed in fire. The men in the outer circle go on dancing, but the women drag him clear of the fire, slap out the sparks in his hair, and lay him on the ground where he lies writhing and moaning in a trance. The women resume their circle and continue singing.

Soon the medicine man gets up. He goes over to the women and touches each in turn, to draw out the evil spirits. After each touch he utters a piercing shriek: the evil has come out. Some of the women faint. People fuss round, and blow into the women's nostrils, mouths, navels, ears. And they spit the strong-smelling juice of a chewed tree root into their faces.

At dawn everyone tumbles into sleep. Only the smouldering fire and the patterned prints of the dancers' feet remain.

The sad thing is that the Bushmen have altogether abandoned their most highly-developed and characteristic art of painting and engraving. You can trace the migrations or former spread of the Bushmen throughout Africa by the rocks and the cave-walls which they adorned. Their work was colorful, naturalistic, and exquisite by any standard. The artists recorded the animals which were their neighbors and their food; many of the paintings also show cattle-raids, dances, and magical or mythological scenes of human figures with animal heads. There are no more Bushman painters; yet as a people they stubbornly survive.

121

Peoples of the Okavango river
southern Africa

In 1858 Charles John Andersson, an explorer, led an expedition into the unmapped interior of the 'dark continent'. He was searching for a river which natives had told him flowed westwards, from Africa's heart to the Atlantic ocean. The expedition took him through the arid lands of what is now South-west Africa, and among the Bushmen, the survivors of a stone-age people who had once dominated the whole of southern Africa. Then, at last, he came upon the river he sought. 'Catching a glimpse of an immense sheet of water in the distance,' he wrote 'my anticipation was realized to its utmost. Twenty minutes more brought us to the banks of a truly noble river, at this point at least 200 yards wide.' But the river was not quite what he expected, for it flowed east-wards towards the heart of the continent, not west. The natives of that region who called themselves the Ovaquan-gari, called the river the Okavango. Only later was it realised that the Okavango was the river which ran into the vast inland swamps of Botswana, to the south east.

The Okavango river has its headwaters many hundreds of miles to the north, in Angola. Two hundred miles from its source it runs into the sandveldt of the Kalahari

123

On their way to the Okavango
river for a day's fishing,
women carry dip trays to
catch fish, the children
carry their own rods.

On the Okavango, one of the only three rivers of South-west Africa, the Andara Roman Catholic mission hold their annual procession.

through which it flows for another 800 miles until it reaches the Okavango swamp where it is lost in a hundred watercourses between the tall cliffs of reeds and rushes. There the bush and sandveldt vanish. Nothing solid is left in sight, only the world of grass and water and a restless draught drawn by the furnace of the surrounding desert.

Andersson had discovered the river and its name, and he also came to know a little of the people who called themselves the Ovaquangari. It is uncertain whether they had seen a white man before and on his approach a general panic ensued. He wrote that 'the women and children set up a most piteous howl, and the men ran about shouting like maniacs. Each village, or rather homestead, was invariably within easy hail of its neighbor; our sudden arrival therefore was announced throughout the country with almost the same speed as a telegram would convey a message.' All the villages and cultivated lands of the Ovaquangari were situated on the north bank of the river. There were many canoes and a number of these were eventually paddled across. The men were tall and their bodies were thickly covered with grease and ocher. Some of the more important and wealthier men also hung their bodies with iron and bead ornaments. They spoke a language that was apparently identical to that spoken by the Ovambo people in the west.

The Ovaquangari gave Andersson and his men several baskets of millet, some maize, pumpkins and a cow. Then came an invitation from the great chief of the Ovaquangari who lived some distance away along the river. But they were reluctant to give him a canoe, saying he should go on foot. The chief's influence, to Andersson's surprise, was limited. Only after much determined language did he procure a canoe for the journey to the chief.

The river flowed fast. Often the paddlers would draw the canoe into the side among the reeds and shallows to avoid hippopotamuses. And then twenty or thirty other heads would appear from the bush to gaze at the strange white man. Occasionally small islands emerged from the stream. These were favorite resorts of the crocodiles and hippopotamuses. On each side of the river there rose the high sides of the valley. The higher parts were covered in thick forest, in contrast to the lower parts where maize and millet grew interspersed with acacia. But still only the north side of the river was extensively cultivated.

The chief's village was little different from those upriver. There were a great number of low huts, built of wattle and daub and roofed with thatch so that they resembled bee-hives. They were all crowded into a confined space, but each hut was partitioned from its neighbor by a circular fence of split wood and mattings. In the center was a kind of courtyard which was used for village gatherings. Andersson wrote of the villagers 'Like the Ovambo, the Ovaquangari engage in agricultural pursuits and ply many trades . . . They manufacture

Many of the Okavango tribes share rituals and traditions with other South-west African tribes: frog dancing is also a custom among the Herero.

Like all women of the Okavango, this mother wants her hair to look straight and long, so she wears a wig of sisal, greased and plaited.

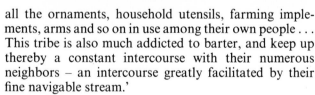

all the ornaments, household utensils, farming implements, arms and so on in use among their own people . . . This tribe is also much addicted to barter, and keep up thereby a constant intercourse with their numerous neighbors – an intercourse greatly facilitated by their fine navigable stream.'

The Okavango river is undoubtedly a finely navigable stream, one of only three in the whole of South-west Africa. It runs through the heart of a region of southern Angola and northern South-west Africa which is populated by the south-western Bantu people. To the south, in the vast expanses of the Kalahari desert, Bushmen and Hottentots live – the tribes which the Bantu overran and are now dying out. And it was from the east, by way of the Okavango river, that these Bantu tribes like the Ovaquangari acquired cattle and the knowledge of dairy farming.

Andersson's observations of one tribe might easily apply today to twenty or even fifty of this region. They fish in the river and on the flood plains where fish are trapped as the water recedes. They work in the fields with hoes, growing millet and maize – crops which are their staple diet (though maize is a relative new comer). They keep cattle, goats and dogs, animals which only recently have been joined by chickens and pigs. Cattle are no less important now than they were a century ago. Not only do cattle yield milk and butter, they also confer prestige and demonstrate a man's wealth. Marriage payments are made with cattle and among many tribes north of the river, every household keeps two sacred cows, one presented by a man's father, the other by his mother's brother. These sacred cows are dedicated to paternal and maternal ancestors.

The villages which Andersson observed are common throughout this region. Among many tribes the central open space, around which the family compounds are built, is used as a cattle corral. But elsewhere this court-yard has a council house building and the chief's residence. The chief's title is hereditary and he governs with the help of a council of elders. He is the headman of a small state and collects tribute from other villages. Many of the tribes in the Okavango region still keep slaves, just as Andersson noted among the Ovaquangari. And the men may have several wives. One of the ambitions among women along the Okavango is to have long straight hair. To imitate this they use wild sisal, plaited and rolled into long strands and then smeared with grease and ocher. This was something Andersson could not fail to note. 'With their crisp woolly hair standing erect in little tangled knots' he wrote 'they might have been reckoned good models for the Furies.'

This is a part of Africa in which life for most African villagers follows the old patterns of agriculture and raising cattle. To the east, where the river runs into the Okavango swamp, it is difficult to imagine that anything could possibly change. Here the hippopotamuses and the crocodiles rule the waterways; buffalo rule the low islands that are raised barely ten feet above the streams. The people are different from their neighbors on the veldt and upstream. They came together in the swamps not by choice, but to escape destruction at the hands of the Matabele in the time of Africa's great troubles in the past. Part Bushman and part Bantu, they live a life of partial seclusion interrupted only by the drone of a plane far above. The planes are mostly those now used to transport other Africans to and from the mines. For the swamp people two-man dugout canoes are the only means of transport. Doctors visit parts of the swamp only once every two or three years. The need for even the simplest medicines is overwhelming. Children catch eye infections which unless treated quickly leave their vision permanently impaired. Many of the small faces have deep scars at the temples and cheeks where witch-doctors cut into the flesh to let out the evil spirits. And then there is the malaria and sleeping-sickness. In this part of Africa a hundred years have brought few changes. 125

Hottentots
South-west Africa

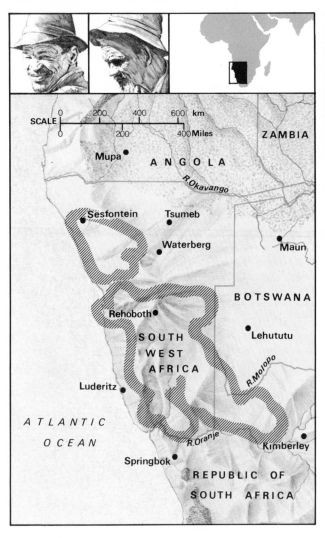

Very few Hottentots live today in the traditional way. Most of them have become urban people, forming part of the group called Cape Colored. A few live on specially provided homelands, and others may live undisturbed in remote places. In 1652 a newly arrived Dutch settler would have had no difficulty in identifying a Hottentot. They were one of two indigenous groups of small yellow-skinned people. They were nomadic cattle breeders, tiny but fierce, with a more complex economy and social organization than the other indigenous group, the Bushmen, whom in some ways they resembled. Both peoples had mongoloid appearances, and the concentration of fat on the buttocks and thighs that is called *steatopygy*. Both peoples were hardy and nomadic, and brave hunters, and both spoke languages with clicking sounds in them. But the Hottentots had peppercorn hair, and they were slightly fatter and taller than the hungry Bushmen who lived from hand to mouth. The Hottentots were pastoralists, owners of fat-

126

The Hottentot way of life is
fast disappearing, but on
reserves some part-white
descendants preserve
their Hottentot identity.

The Reheboth, descendants of
settlers and Hottentots are
proud of their Dutch blood
and like to wear 19th century
costume, like this paper cap.

This woman's figure shows
traces of steatopygy, or
characteristic fat storing,
which she may owe to
her Hottentot blood.

tailed sheep and cattle, which had for them an enormous personal and almost mythical significance, as well as providing a stability that the Bushmen never had. They also had more possessions, like their huge three gallon cooking pots, and probably knew how to smelt iron.

In those days and until recently the tight-knit Hottentot tribes were like the Mongols of Genghis Khan, endlessly feuding, training their treasured cattle to charge the enemy in battle with their heads down. In the late 19th century, for example, the Hottentots had a long and bitter war with the Herero. They even came occasionally to blows with the peaceful Bushmen, who sometimes tracked and killed Hottentot cattle when game was scarce. But normally relations with their neighbors were peaceful, and they often intermarried with them.

Early 20th century observers have seen the Hottentots living much as they did when the whites came to the Cape in the 17th century. All four groups (the Nama, the Kora, the Gringa and the Gona) built beehive-shaped huts by planting sticks about a foot deep in the ground in a circle, and bending them to meet at a point in the center, and covering them with carefully woven rush mats, which swelled whenever it rained into an absolutely air-tight covering. The huts were arranged in circles or kraals, around an area which effectively formed a pen. The huts were portable, and when the time came for the tribe to move on, they were loaded with cooking pots and hunting equipment onto the family's oxen, which provided trans-

port as well as milk and meat. Some Hottentot cattle were even used as sheep dogs, rounding up sheep and younger cattle. They would obey commands from very long distances.

The women looked after the cattle and did most of the work except for hunting. They were skilled potters and produced enormous cooking pots and bowls. Like the Bushmen the Hottentots owned possessions in common: a 19th century observer, firmly committed to individual enterprise and competition wrote disapprovingly that as the Hottentots always shared their food and good fortune equally, no one person ever got ahead.

This is not to say that everyone has the same status. This depended largely on generation, and Hottentot languages to this day include many terms of respect for position. Family organization was patrilineal, and a special position was reserved for the mother's brother, whose status was as high as that of grandparents and ancestors. Except for his children, all the children born of his generation within his family were considered brothers and sisters. Families very often came to love their slaves or servants and eventually to call them brother or sister. Hottentot tribes were basically family units linked with each other through the mother's brother.

The judicial system was as simple as the kinship system. The *tata-gu,* the fathers, acted on a council of which the eldest and most respected was the *tata-b,* who was particularly powerful in times of war. Outside the family and

Generations of intermarriage means some Reheboth could pass for Boers, others for Hottentots; many more have inherited mixed traits.

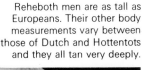

Reheboth men are as tall as Europeans. Their other body measurements vary between those of Dutch and Hottentots and they all tan very deeply.

tribe, but never within, the death penalty was inflicted for any slight without fear of retribution.

Obviously cattle provided much of the Hottentot's diet but they also ate maize, yams, wild roots, game, and fish which they speared. They were brave hunters and often faced lions alone, armed only with an *assegai*. They smoked hemp called dakka, which was gradually replaced with tobacco from white men and the Bantu.

Their rites of passage were relatively simple, by comparison with other African peoples. Boys were circumcised at nine or ten, incest was taboo and women were only married with their consent, and a bride-price was settled by the bride-groom and future father-in-law. Then, and until recently, the Hottentots were polygamous. At birth a baby was smeared with cow dung with rites of purification, and the placenta was burnt. At death corpses were sprinkled with blood, sewn up in rush mats and buried in a sitting position, facing east on an excavation on one side of the grave, so that earth was not thrown on a corpse when the grave was filled up. Before the Hottentots accepted Christianity they probably believed in the after-life of the spirit; and certainly their languages, which are widely spoken today, include various references to deities. God was a figure like the Odin of Norse myth, called Father and Thunderer, with an opponent resembling Loki, called the Destroyer or the Whirlwind.

The white settlers assimilated the Hottentots as servants and laborers and later converted them to Christianity. The Hottentots intermarried with Bantu slaves imported to southern Africa from other parts of the continent, with indentured Asian laborers, and, most confusingly for the anthropologist, with the Bushmen. In this way they began to lose not only their traditional ways, but their distinctive appearance. Today although there are now about 100,000 people in southern Africa who speak one or other of the Hottentot dialects, most

Hottentots are westernized urban workers and the vast majority are of the mixed group called Cape Colored.

Anthropologists have argued a great deal about the Hottentots' origins, their old way of life, and simply what it means to be a Hottentot. Many have identified them with the Bushmen, calling both peoples Khoisan, from a verb meaning 'to gather'. And then Hottentot is almost a term of abuse, and so is rarely used. Only their language, the subject of much recent research, remains a distinctive means of identifying the Hottentots.

The Nama are today probably the purest representatives of the original groups. But there is one group of people of Hottentot origin which has kept its identity in a particularly odd way. The Rehoboth and the Gringas Bastaards, as they proudly call themselves, are the descendants of Hottentots and white settlers. They are proud of their white blood, which means that they are not 'native', and are above Kaffir work and manual labor. The Rehoboth Bastaards live in a reserve 700 miles north of Cape Town. There are clearly Dutch elements in their way of life particularly in the way they dress. They ardently support apartheid of an idiosyncratic sort, and keep themselves apart from Bantu and Cape Colored. For example when apartheid was introduced to the Rehoboth reserve in the 1950s, the Bastaards preferred to lose their white community, and asked it to go, rather than share the non-European post-office and shop counters with 'natives'.

Glossary to the peoples of southern Africa and Madagascar

BANTU

The Bantu tribes of southern Africa are descended from the negroid people who emerged from the equatorial rain forests of Central Africa and spread east and south. Several hundred tribes are united by languages of the Bantu family but it is difficult to identify a physical type that is exclusively Bantu. Essentially they are negroes who have mixed with Hamitic, negrillo and Bushmen types. The Hamitic strain is visible in the Zulu while many Swazi are almost as black as the pure West African negroes. Africanists usually divide the Bantu into linguistic and cultural zones and speak of certain groups of tribes as belonging to the central Bantu, to the middle Zambezi Bantu or to the south-western Bantu. These people were able to displace the Khoisans and gain control of southern Africa by their superior technology and their well-developed political organization.

EUROPEANS

The first Europeans to arrive in the area were the Portuguese. They landed in Africa on their way to India and the East Indies during the 15th century and soon established their colonies along the coast of what are now their overseas territories of Angola and Mozambique. The settlement of the Cape was left to the Dutch who arrived in the middle of the 17th century. They were joined by some Huguenots. Together they spread through the area that is today known as South Africa. They were followed by the British who settled in large numbers during the 18th, 19th and 20th centuries. A significant population of Jews has been well established since the turn of the century. The various white racial groups have kept relatively distinct.

ASIANS

The Asians who constitute a large and economically significant minority are descended in part from Malays who were brought in as servants of the Dutch, but mainly from Indians who came in under Britain's indentured immigration scheme in the 19th and early 20th centuries.

COLOREDS

There is in southern Africa a large population of what is loosely termed coloreds. These are people of mixed white and Hottentot or Bantu origin who, because they fit into neither European nor tribal society, are generally considered to form a separate and distinguishable subculture.

MALAGASY

In contrast with the mainland, Madagascar has a population that is surprisingly homogenous in language and culture. The ethnic make-up of the Malagasy, on the other hand, is a complex mixture of physical types – negroid, mongoloid, and caucasoid. All of the island's inhabitants came as migrants. Sea-going Indonesians, who probably landed around 1,000 BC were undoubtely the first settlers. They account for the strong mongoloid element and for the Malayo-Polynesian languages that are still spoken in Madagascar. Much later, in the 12th century the Arabs came. They settled in the south-east and introduced the Arab and Islamic elements that are still clearly present today. They also imported large numbers of negro slaves from southern Africa.

KHOISANS

The entire area of what is now South Africa, South-west Africa (Namibia), Botswana, Lesotho and Swaziland as well as portions of Angola, Zambia and Rhodesia was once the home of Khoisan-speaking aborigines. These were stone-age men who led a nomadic existence and lived by hunting wild animals and gathering edible fruit, roots, nuts and honey. They had very few possessions and their technology was rudimentary. A wandering way of life made it impossible for them to consolidate from the north and European settlers from the east and the south were able to deprive them of virtually all desirable land. These ancient inhabitants of southern Africa now number little more than 100,000. Most are serfs to the more sophisticated Bantu tribesmen. Those few who preserve their ancient way of life are now confined to inhospitable areas in South-west Africa, the Kalahari desert and the Okavango swamp region. These survivors from the past fall into three distinct groups: the Bushmen, the Hottentots, and the Bergdama.

The Bushmen are short people, rarely taller than 5 feet. Their skin is yellowish-brown and has a parched look. Even young adults are wrinkled. The head is usually of medium to narrow width and is covered in very tight spirals of short black hair. The eyes are narrow, almost mongoloid. A broad nose contrasts with thin lips and a pointed chin. The body is slender and agile.

The Hottentots tend to be 4 to 5 inches taller than the Bushmen and have narrower heads and noses. Observers have often remarked upon the prominence of Hottentots' buttocks which are particularly large in the women. This physical trait is shared with the Bushmen and is due to a slight curvature of the lower spine. Culturally they differ from their Bushmen cousins because they have adopted a pastoral way of life and herd cattle obtained from the south-western Bantu. But for many generations they intermarried with Europeans and Bantu and most now form part of the large, detribalized mixed-blood population known as Cape Colored.

The Bergdama are more akin to negroes than to Bushmen in appearance. But culturally and linguistically they belong with the Bushmen and Hottentots. They are thought to be the most primitive negroes in Africa apart from the Congo pygmies. Long enslaved by the Hottentots and assimilated into Bantu groups they are among the vanishing peoples of Africa.

From the 16th century onwards Europeans and Africans began to move into southern Africa already inhabited by Bushmen and Hottentots. The Bantu were migrating southwards as the Europeans, having discovered the sea route to the east and revictualling stations on the south coast, were beginning to settle the hinterland. Under powerful leaders the Bantu states of Zulu, Matabele and Kolokolo began to expand and finding the south of the country occupied by Boers they moved back north into Zambia and Rhodesia. Meanwhile the Boers rebelling against the British on the coast began the Great Trek in 1836 which led them to settle in the Orange Free State and the Transvaal.

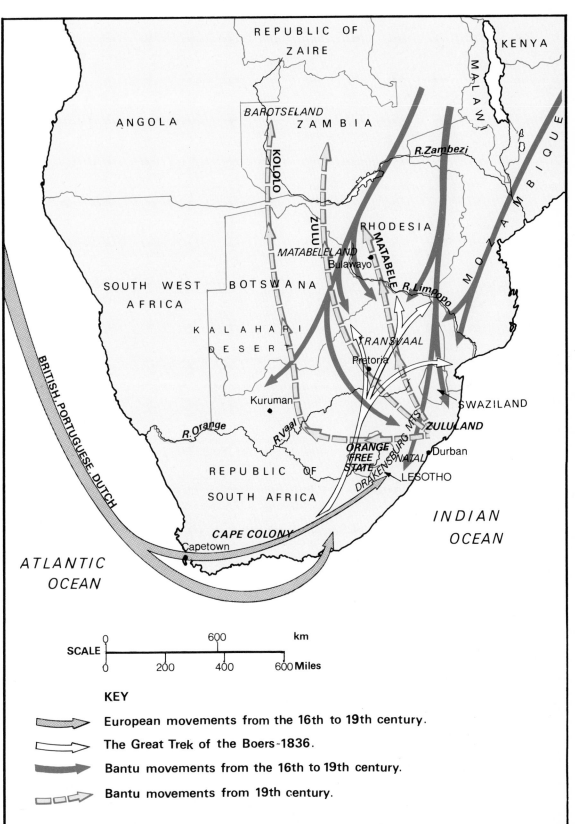

SCALE

| 0 | | 600 | km |

| 0 | 200 | 400 | 600 Miles |

KEY

European movements from the 16th to 19th century.

The Great Trek of the Boers - 1836.

Bantu movements from the 16th to 19th century.

Bantu movements from 19th century.

AFRIKANERS *Population:* 2 million. Language: Afrikaans. The Afrikaners are the dominant group in South Africa, descendants of people who came from Europe, mainly from Holland, during and after the 17th century. Afrikaans is derived from Dutch. Most Afrikaners were farmers in the hinterland around Cape Town until, fretting under British authority, they made their exodus in 1837, known as the Great Trek. Some 10,000 Boers, as they then called themselves, moved north-east into the Transvaal and Natal in wagons drawn largely by oxen, clashing with the recently established African tribes of the area. After a struggle for dominance which culminated in the Boer wars, won by the British in 1902, the Afrikaners remained under British rule until 1910, and under strong British influence until the National Party came into power in 1948. The Nationalists instituted and upheld the policy of *apartheid* – separate development of races. Today the Afrikaners farm cattle and sheep, many hold positions in the civil and military services. More and more are becoming urban workers; but only since the 1950s have some become prominent in big business. Most are adherents of the (Calvinist) Dutch Reformed Church. **(pages 62-65)**

AMBO *Population:* 175,000. Language: Bantu. The Ambo are culturally and linguistically related to the Herero (q.v.) and Ovimbundu (q.v.). Their country is on both sides of the upper Kunene River on the border of Angola and South-west Africa. Ovamboland consists of a vast expanse of white sand sparsely covered with grass and acacia inundated, between May and July, with torrential rains. For much of the rest of the year it is a parched plain, pitted here and there by wells and water holes. The Ambo grow sorghum and millet on beds of earth and cow dung, which they build up above the level of the plain. They keep cattle under difficult conditions more as a store of wealth and for prestige than for food. Their settlements are either small villages or dispersed hamlets of beehive-shaped dwellings made of saplings covered by grass. Government at the local level rests in the hands of hereditary headmen. The whole tribe, however recognizes the authority of a divine king who rules with the queen-mother. The king's chief wife tends a sacred fire which is kindled at his installation and extinguished at his death. The ruler is said to possess supernatural powers and is expected to perform rites to assure good crops and the health of his people.

Blacksmiths occupy a special role in this society as do diviners. Religion centers on the royal fire cult and on worship of the ancestors.

ANTAIFASY *Population:* 20,000. Language: Malagasy (Malayo-Polynesian). The Antaifasy inhabit parts of eastern Madagascar around Farafangana. Predominantly wet-rice cultivators, those who live along the coast also do a certain amount of fishing. The tribe is divided into three named clans each led by a 'king' who acts as chief celebrant in the ancestor cult. The dead are buried in collective tombs.

ANTAIMORO *Population:* 240,000. Language: Malagasy (Malayo-Polynesian). The Antaimoro occupy an area along the south-east coast of Madagascar in the region of Manakara and Vohipeno. They came under strong Islamic influence around the 13th century and still retain an unorthodox form of Islam: they abstain from pork, for example and observe Muslim fast days. But their knowledge of Islamic theology is scant. They learned to apply Arabic script to Malagasy and preserve manuscripts containing magic formulae and historical records. Once sea-going merchants, they have now been reduced to tending rice and coffee plantations. They build their huts on piles. The Antaimoro operate an elaborate caste system that consists of nobles, priests, free men, slaves and untouchables. They are also organized into age groups. The society is held together by the universal fear of being refused burial in their collective tombs.

ANTAISAKA *Population:* 345,000. Language: Malagasy (Malayo-Polynesian). The Antaisaka live on the south-east coast of Madagascar in the area between Farafangana and Vangaindrano, but many have migrated further south. Today large numbers of them have migrated to other parts of the island as wage laborers. It has been estimated that at any one time half the able-bodied men might be away earning enough money to buy oxen with which to return to their tribal land. They live in densely packed villages and build their huts on piles. They are primarily wet-rice cultivators. They have a royal tomb cult and bury their dead twice: first in a provisional grave and two or three years later in permanent tombs.

ANTANDROY *Population:* 210,000. Language: Malagasy (Malayo-Polynesian). The Antandroy live in small villages at the arid southern end of Madagascar. Most are pastoral cattle herders who also cultivate rice and do some fishing. They have that obsession with cattle that is so common in East Africa. Tall and tough, they managed to escape domination by the Merina (q.v.) at a time most other Malagasy tribes were subjugated. In 1931 they suffered a severe famine as a result of which a great number of them migrated to other parts of the island. In recent years they have provided much of the unskilled labor on large plantations. At one time they were known for their tattoos but this form of bodily adornment is rapidly disappearing. Antandroy women occupy an inferior position in society. The Antandroy tomb cult involves placing carved wooden vessels in cemeteries to commemorate those who died while away from the tribal territory.

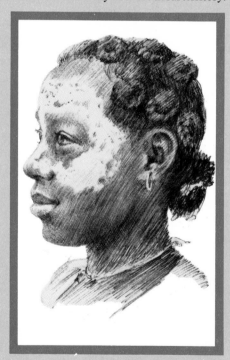

ANTANKARANA *Population:* 38,000. Language: Malagasy (Malayo-Polynesian). The Antankarana live in the northern part of the island of Madagascar. Their dwellings are constructed on piles. They are tall people who live a relatively sedentary way of life and subsist mainly by breeding cattle. Those that live along the coast are often good sailors and fishermen. This society has been influenced

by Islam although they remain ancestor worshippers. They have a royal family and the traces of Islamic culture are most visible in their court procedure and in the dress worn by royalty.
(pages 72-75)

BARA *Population:* 210,000. Language: Malagasy (Malayo-Polynesian). The Bara occupy the lower plateaux of southern Madagascar and the north of the area belonging to the Mahafaly (q.v.) and the Antandroy (q.v.). They live in rectangular mud-walled huts and pursue a form of nomadic pastoralism. Their overriding attachment to cattle is as much sentimental as it is economic. Each man's greatest ambition is to own the largest possible herd of cows. They are aggressive and take pride in stealing cattle from neighboring groups. Here, as among the Antandroy (q.v.), women have an inferior position. A woman is only allowed to inherit movable property. Lineage and family solidarity is strong. Polygamy on a large scale survived longer here than in most other parts of the island. The Bara are known for their elaborate funeral ceremonies: as in many other Malagasy societies temporary burial of the dead precedes a final transfer to the family tomb. They believe in life-giving spirits that manifest themselves under certain trees.

BASUTO (see SOTHO)

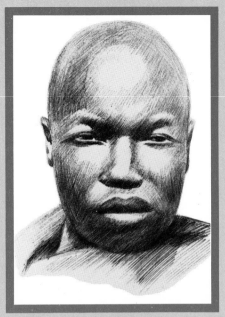

BATHONGA *Population:* 200,000-300,000. Language: Bantu. Culturally and linguistically the Bathonga form part of the Thonga (q.v.) tribal group. The bulk of the population lives on the border of Transvaal and Mozambique just north of Swaziland in the Kruger National Park. They live in a land of savanna and forests in which husbandry and agriculture are of equal economic importance. Their staples are millet and maize which they grind up and eat as a porridge. They hunt and fish and keep cattle for marriage payments and to settle the fines that result from adultery, murder and other offenses. They eat a little chicken and goat meat but rarely eat beef. They trace descent through the father's family but attach great importance to the role of mother's brother. Maternal uncles are important in the elaborate ceremonies that accompany puberty and marriage. Boys are subjected to painful ordeals to mark their transition to manhood which include beatings, starvation and circumcision endured in special forest camps where they remain secluded for up to three months. The Bathonga live in dispersed villages each associated with a lineage or family. For centuries they have had elaborate political institutions and paramount chiefs whose welfare is associated with the well-being of the entire people. They have a concept of a Supreme Being but their beliefs center around the ancestors. They take many precautions against witchcraft and sorcery.

BERGDAMA *Population:* 30,000. Language: Khoisan. The Bergdama live in a region of South-west Africa between Windhoek and Grootfontein, in an area shared by the more numerous Herero (q.v.) and Nama Hottentots (q.v.) with whom the Bergdama are mixed. The few who have preserved their original mode of life subsist almost entirely by hunting and gathering. But most of them have come under the sway of the Hottentots or Herero whom they serve as herdsmen and servants. The surviving hunters and gatherers have deliberately rejected a more settled way of life. Their possessions are few – no more, in fact than can easily be carried from camp to camp. Tools and implements, like those of the Bushmen (q.v.) are of the most rudimentary kind. They do not store food, but gather berries and edible roots daily, and distribute and eat small game soon after it is killed. They are organized into small independent units. Each local group will consist of a patriarchal family and perhaps a handful of relatives who have placed themselves under the protection of its head. Bergdama camps are grouped shelters made of tied grass or reeds, most of them really no more than windbreaks. These people differ from other Khoisans in their ceremonial life. Each little group has its own sacred fire which must never be allowed to go out. It is guarded night and day by the older men and all good and evil hangs upon protecting the fire from the impurities caused by misconduct.

BETSILEO *Population:* 700,000. Language: Malagasy (Malayo-Polynesian). The Betsileo live in the high plateaux of central Madagascar, south of the Mania river. Meticulous cultivators of rice, they are known for their deep attachment to the soil, their endurance and their pacifism. They are somewhat shorter and stockier than most of their cattle-herding neighbors. Wood carvers and traders, they have developed an elaborate market system. Today they are all Christians, mainly Catholics, but traces of pre-Christian times survive in their tomb cults and in their belief in the earthly sojourn of souls after death.

BETSIMISARAKA *Population:* 800,000. Language: Malagasy (Malayo-Polynesian). The Betsimisaraka are forest people who live along the eastern coast of Madagascar between Sambava and Nosy-Varika. They build their huts in scattered clusters over a

133

wide area. At one time their little villages were stockaded. Climatic conditions make cattle-raising impractical. They are mainly cultivators of rice, coffee and cassava. There is evidence that they were once potters but that they lost the art. Today most of their containers are made of gourds. The women still wear the primitive raffia skirts of former days. They have collective family tombs and practise ancestor worship. The cult of the ancestors is presided over by a priestly caste. They believe in a supreme god and a number of minor deities that personify natural phenomena.

BRITISH *Population:* 1.5 million. Language: English. The British live mainly in South Africa and Rhodesia. In Rhodesia most are farmers, businessmen and industrialists. In South Africa, where they number 1,225,000, they tend to be engaged in business, industry and the professions, rather than agriculture. Few hold positions in the government or the military or civil services. The first 5,000 British settlers went to South Africa in 1820, succeeded later by an influx of engineers, miners and businessmen who followed the discovery of gold and diamonds in quantity in the latter part of the century. After the Boer War in 1899-1902 (see Afrikaners), which the British won, many ex-soldiers stayed, more settlers went out to South Africa and through the Union of South Africa the British

consolidated their control of the country. Their political influence was exerted through the United Party, led by the Afrikaner Jan Smuts, until the all-Afrikaner National Party came into power in 1948; yet since South Africa parted company with the British Commonwealth over the Nationalists' apartheid policy in 1961, and became a republic, the two major white races have, if anything, got on better. Yet British and Afrikaners still tend not to intermarry, and most South Africans of British stock cannot speak Afrikaans although it is the national language.

BUSHMEN *Population:* 55,000. Language: Khoisan. Of the many small tribes of Bushmen the best known are the Koroca who occupy a tiny strip of land on the south-west coast of Angola, the Naron and the Kung of the central Kalahari Desert of South-west Africa and the Neikum of the southern part of the Kalahari Desert. Small bands, rarely numbering more than twenty, still manage to lead a simple and unaffected way of life on the marshland left to them by the more powerful Bantu and European invaders. They live by hunting and gathering, with the men killing game and the women dedicated to collecting wild vegetable foods. They eat a great variety of things but not, as is often assumed, just anything which is edible. But they are particularly fond of all kinds of birds and fish and their diet also includes anteaters, tortoises, porcupines, bullfrogs, snakes, lizards, various insects such as locusts, scorpions, young bees, termites, flying ants and ants' eggs. But they reject baboons, because they resemble men, and hyenas, because they feed on corpses. Much of their food is eaten raw.

The band is highly mobile and tends to move camp more often than the search for food necessitates. Three or four families move freely through a territory that they regard as their own hunting ground. They will not move out of this territory without securing the permission of an adjoining group. There are no chiefs, but older men and skilled hunters have considerable influence in directing day-to-day life. The only personal property they recognize is that which can be carried – such as clothing, ornaments, food scrapers and digging sticks. Bushman technology is of the simplest kind. They hunt with bows and poison-tipped arrows and with throwing sticks, pitfalls and snares of all kinds. Their encampments are temporary and, whenever they can, they make use of natural shelters like caves, but they usually construct

windbreaks consisting of semi-circles of saplings set in the ground tied together, fastened at the top and covered with grass or reed matting. The Bushman family of a man, his wife and children, is the most enduring social unit. There are no extended families, and polygamy, while not forbidden, is hardly ever practised. At marriage, the man usually gives the bride's parents a few small gifts (typically, of meat) and works for them for a short period. The newly-wed couple may choose to live with the husband's people; the wife's people, or join another group altogether.

There is no Bushman religion as such. They never believe that death is by natural causes. They all fear sorcery and whenever someone dies the band moves to another camp. Bushmen believe in an after-life in which they will feed on locusts and honey. The practice of severing a finger at the first joint, common to some groups, is thought to mark those destined for life-after-death.
(pages 114-121)

CAPE COLOREDS *Population:* 1,805,000. Languages: Afrikaans, English. The Cape Coloreds live in South Africa. They are descended from the union of Dutch and Huguenot settlers with the indigenous Hottentots and, to a lesser extent, imported Bantu and Malay slaves. Some of their colored ancestors were free, and all were liberated by 1837. The Cape Coloreds today are tradesmen, artisans and businessmen. In the social hierarchy of South Africa they rank immediately below the whites. Until the apartheid laws became stricter those who had white physical characteristics often used to 'pass' as whites.

CHOKWE *Population:* 510,000. Language: Bantu. Most Chokwe live where the three countries of Angola, Zambia and Zaïre meet, but they are in fact dispersed over a wide area. Much of their territory is shared with Ovimbundu tribesmen. The northern Chokwe gain their livelihood mainly from hunting although they also practise agriculture. The southern and central Chokwe are farmers who place little importance on hunting. They live in bush country that is rugged and undulating. The soil is generally poor. Descent is traced through the mother's family and most young children go to live with their mother's brothers when they are about six years old. It is from the maternal uncle that property is inherited. Villages are of two types. In the north clusters of huts, built of

grass or straw, are frequently moved. In the south most people build solid mud huts. Settlements are small and tend to be 5 to 15 miles apart. Cattle is highly valued but only chiefs can afford large herds. The presence of the tsetse fly makes animal husbandry very precarious. The Chokwe have never had a paramount chief. Traditionally they are ruled by several independent high chiefs each of whom maintains a court and separate administration. They believe in a Supreme Being associated with rain, thunder and lightning. They also worship the ancestors.
(pages 104-107)

CHOPI *Population:* 75,000. Language: Bantu. The Chopi form a part of the culturally homogeneous Thonga (q.v.) nation. They are concentrated along a strip of coastal Mozambique around Inhambane. The proximity of tropical rain forest and the tsetse fly makes it difficult to keep cattle. They derive their living principally from the cultivation of maize and kafir corn. Their villages tend to be small – no more than a dozen to twenty families living together. Most of the men in a village or hamlet will claim descent from a common ancestor. Unlike other Bantu tribes in the area they do not cluster their dwellings around a corral in which cows are kept. Chopi huts of wattle and daub are usually grouped around a sacred tree. Any damage sustained by the tree by disease or lightning, for instance, is interpreted as an evil omen that will lead to the abandonment of the village. They worship the ancestors and practise a taboo that forbids women to come in contact with cattle.

COMORIANS *Population:* 100,000. Language: Swahili. The Comorians inhabit the Comoro Islands, a small archipelago – a quarter the size of Corsica – in the Indian Ocean about 150 miles east of northern Mozambique. The four islands in the archipelago are Grande Comore, Anjouan, Mohéli and Mayotte. It is thought that the islands may have been uninhabited until the 5th or 6th century AD. Many believe that the original settlers came from Indonesia, Malaysia, or Polynesia, having been blown across the Indian Ocean in their outrigger canoes during the April to November monsoon. But apart from outrigger canoes there is little in the culture of the Comoro islands to indicate early Asian influence.

By the 10th century there were Arabs trading there and the African immigrants had come from the mainland. The Comoro Islands were conquered by Shirazi Muslims in the 16th century and Islam was established as the official religion. The Shirazi thought themselves superior to the early Arab traders and Africans and immediately set up small sultanates which exist to this day. The Islamic élite rules over the negroes and poorer Muslims. The negroes are descended from slaves and freemen. Until recently there were distinct Arab, freemen and slave quarters in all towns. The Comorians' economy depends largely on coconuts and bananas. There is considerable Malagasy influence from the east and Bantu influence from the African mainland. But the Comoro Islands are a Muslim country although still part of France. (The French settled there from the last century). Today, as in the 16th century, they represent the southernmost extremity of the Islamic world.

HERERO *Population:* 60,000. Language: Bantu. Most Herero live between the Etosha Pan of South-west Africa and the Cubango river in Angola. About one third live inside Angola. The Herero were once among the richest of the Bantu cattle-keeping people. In 1904, however, they began waging a long war against the Germans which resulted in defeat and impoverishment. Today they are the only major Bantu group who have totally abandoned agriculture in order to pursue an independent pastoral nomadic life. Much of their land is desert and the search for water and grass requires them to move in small bands with their cows. Milk foods, and especially sour milk, are their staples. Settlements are small and consist of a circle of huts, often surrounded by a thorn fence, with a corral in the center. Certain cows are considered sacred and are associated in a special way with the ancestors. Fishing is done by all. Hunting is entrusted to a specially initiated group of men. Pottery is the exclusive province of women. Both men and women are allowed to tend cows. This contrasts with the practice of most other Bantu tribes who impose a cattle taboo on their females. Women mutilate their genitals for aesthetic reasons: the outer fold of the vagina is perforated and a stone attached by a piece of twine in order to elongate the vulva. This custom is however disappearing.
(pages 108-113)

HOTTENTOT *Population:* 35,000. Language: Khoisan. Most Hottentots are found between the Orange river and the Cape. So many of them have mixed with Europeans that they have come to form a principal component in South Africa's colored population. Of the few small Hottentot tribes that have survived to the present day, the Nama are the best known and documented. The Nama Hottentots are concentrated in the area south of the Orange river and north of Brandvlei. These people differ from the other Khoisan groups in that they have for centuries led pastoral lives. They breed herds of long-horned cows and fat-tailed sheep. Cattle are very rarely slaughtered for food.

The staple food is sour milk which is prepared by mixing it with vegetable substance of some kind. Green leaves of ebony trees, for instance, are chewed and spat into fresh milk to produce a thick edible substance. What meat they consume is obtained from hunting wild animals and they take pride in the fact that no part of the animal remains uneaten. Everything is prepared by softening and cooking; even the skin is eaten when the hair has been burned off. Vegetable food is collected from the veldt and they are particularly fond of eating various kinds of roots. There are food taboos that differ from area to area. Cattle has great social significance in that cows are given to the wife's family by the husband's family before marriage. In this the Hottentot resemble their Bantu neighbors but, unlike most Bantu, it is the women who milk the cows. The Nama Hottentot are divided into several sub-tribes each of which has its own chief and named territory. Chiefly authority is weak, however, because decisions are taken through a council of elders who act as the chief's advisers. Villages consist of groups of 'beehive' huts covered with reed mats. Settlements are arranged in circular form with an open space in the centre where the cattle are kept at night. The Hottentot are richer in possessions than their Bushman and Bergdama relatives. They smelt iron for implements and weapons. Their beliefs center around the worship of mythical heroes and the personification of natural forces that produce rain. There is no ancestor cult to speak of but the ghosts of the dead are thought to bring sickness and misfortune. Prayers are often addressed to heavenly bodies and especially to the Moon. Finger mutilation, like that practised by the Bushmen, was once very common among Hottentot women but is now disappearing. Similarly there are now very few cases of polygamy. Marriage regulations are stricter

135

than those of the Bushmen and Bergdama. **(pages 126-129)**

ILA *Population:* 40,000. Language: Bantu. The Ila live mainly in the Kafue river basin to the west of Lusaka in Zambia. Much of Ilaland lies at 3,000 feet above sea level. There is abundant rainfall and the soil lends itself to the cultivation of sorghum, millet, eleusine and maize. Agriculture is combined with cattle herding and a good deal of additional food is obtained from gathering wild fruit. In recent years they have derived much of their income from market gardening, stock rearing and wage labor. Most of their villages are small and compact. Low cylindrical huts with thatched roofs are grouped around a central corral for the cattle. The Ila trace descent through the maternal line. An Ila child looks to his mother's brother for his inheritance and takes the name of his mother's people. Marriage is often unstable. Traditionally men allowed their wives to take publicly-recognized lovers from whom the husbands then received regular payments. Although this custom is said to be dying out, desertions and adultery are still more common than in most Bantu societies. There are elaborate puberty rites, particularly for girls. Until recent years it was common to mutilate the teeth by filing and by extraction. The tribe has no centralized political authority. Groups of villages will combine for certain purposes under a headman. The main role of petty chiefs is a ritual one. There is a traditional system of justice that involves trial by ordeal or poison. Witchcraft is punished by death. European administration put an end to traditional punishments in all but the most remote areas. There is a cult of a Supreme Deity associated with rain. They venerate ancestral spirits and attribute crop failure and other misfortunes to sorcerers. Diseases are thought to be caused by contact with certain animals or menstruating women and by the breaking of certain taboos.

INDIANS *Population:* 445,000. Languages: Indian and Pakistani languages – especially Tamil, Hindi, Urdu, Telugu and Gujarati – English, Afrikaans. The Indians (including those descended from families who originated in what is now Pakistan) mostly live around Durban in Natal. They first came to South Africa in the 19th century as indentured laborers for the cane fields, many of them accompanied by their wives. At the end of their five-year period of work they were entitled either to a free passage back to India or to crown lands to the value of their passage. Many elected to stay in South Africa and were joined by others who came as traders, merchants and craftsmen. Some Indians are still employed in the cane fields but many are traders – small shopkeepers or owners of huge trading empires. Many own Indian newspapers or laundries and thousands go into the hotel business. Most are Hindus, but there are about 100,000 Muslims and 35,000 Christians. Gandhi spent 20 years in South Africa from 1893 and it was here, fighting for equal citizenship rights for Indians, that he first began his policy of passive resistance.

KARANGA *Population:* 50,000. Language: Bantu. The Karanga live in the districts of Chilimanzi, Chibi and Victoria in southern Mashonaland which is today a part of Rhodesia. They form a part of the culturally homogeneous Shona nation (q.v.).

KIMBUNDU *Population:* 25,000. Language: Bantu. The Kimbundu live in central Angola's Luanda Province. Their land is a mixture of hilly grassland with clusters of trees and river beds that are dry for much of the year. They keep cows, goats, chickens and a few pigs. Cattle are kept for prestige reasons. They rarely eat beef and never milk their cows except to obtain the butter that they use to anoint their bodies. Their economy rests primarily on slash-and-burn agriculture. The main staples are cassava and maize. The Kimbundu live in small villages surrounded by stockades. Young boys are circumcised as part of their puberty ceremony. Children belong to their mothers' families and young men make their homes in the villages of maternal uncles. Instead of paying the bride-price in cows or goods at marriage, husbands perform a lengthy period of bride service, working for their in-laws. Local chiefs have their own courts and administration but there is no paramount chieftaincy. Slavery and cannibalism survived until relatively recent times. Religion centers on the worship of ancestors.

KONGO *Population:* 2,500,000. Language: Bantu. The Kongo occupy a large terrain that stretches from the Loje river in Angola, east of Ambrizete, to Brazzaville in Zaïre. The land is rugged, but fertile and well watered. Once the Kongo were a powerful nation who impressed the first Portuguese explorers with the complexity of their political institutions. They were ruled by a king – the Manikongo – who made his capital in what is today São Salvador do Congo. Today tribesmen work for Europeans as wage laborers and cultivate the land. Cattle has prestige value but the economy rests on simple slash-and-burn agriculture. The main crops are yams, sweet potato, bananas, maize and cassava. A starchy diet is supplemented by animal proteins derived from hunting and fishing. Descent is traced through one's mother and men will usually live with their maternal uncles. Although the power of the king has virtually disappeared he retains much moral and spiritual control over his people. He is the custodian of a sacred fire and the welfare of the people is thought to depend on his well-being. Christianity was first brought to the Kongo people in the 16th century but has never taken hold completely. Christian symbols are mixed up with traditional ones in Kongo religion.

KOREKORE *Population:* 100,000. Language: Bantu. The Korekore inhabit Rhodesia's northern districts of Lomagundi, Darwin, Mrwea and Mazoe to the north and north-east of Salisbury. They form an important part of the culturally homogenous Shona nation (q.v.).

KOROCA see BUSHMEN

KUNG see BUSHMEN

LAKA *Population:* 150,000. Language: Bantu. It is characteristic of the Laka dialect of Bantu that they retain certain sounds, known as 'clicks' characteristic of the aboriginal Khoisan languages. This indicates the relatively late arrival of the Bantu speakers and their intermarriage with the original inhabitants. The Laka are dispersed over a large area of Transvaal north of Pretoria, South Africa. They are cultivators of maize and herders of cattle. Their staples are maize and milk products. They live in 'beehive' huts of dried grass grouped around a cattle corral. Cattle dung is mixed with earth and used in surfacing buildings and floors. At marriage a substantial bride-price is paid in cows. A man retains absolute rights over his wife and her children even after his death. The widow does not remarry but has intercourse with her husband's younger brother or other close relative. Any children borne as a result of this are ascribed to the dead husband. Worship centers on ancestral spirits.

LOVEDU *Population:* 80,000. Language: Bantu. The Lovedu live in the high grasslands of Transvaal, South Africa. Cultivators of maize and herders of cattle they also derive much of their income from wage labor. They do not impose the usual cattle taboo on females but women do not usually milk cows except in an emergency. Polygamy survived on a large scale longer than it did in many other areas mainly because the women formed a solid front against the Christian missionaries who attempted to impose monogamy. Lovedu women believe that a woman's rights and status can only be protected adequately if she has the support of other wives against her husband. The Lovedu are known for their female 'kings'. Since 1800 the monarchs have been women who have assumed the role of men. They beget children by 'marrying' wives who are then provided with lovers. It is from among the children of these wives that a successor to the throne is chosen. The monarch herself leads a promiscuous sex life and any of her offspring are counted as 'illegitimate' and thus unable to inherit any of her power. The 'king' is expected to commit suicide when she develops any defect and the second monarch did, in fact, kill herself in 1894 when she no longer considered herself fit to rule. This is the only Sotho (q.v.) tribe that keeps slaves. Religion centers on ancestors.

LOZI *Population:* 180,000. Language: Bantu. The Lozi occupy Barotseland, a vast flood-plain of the Upper Zambesi river in Zambia. They cultivate millet, eleusine and maize. They keep cattle and fish. Each community has two villages. One of these is built on an artificial mound in the flood-plain, the other on the edge of the plain. They migrate from the first to the second during the rainy season. The Lozi, like the Sotho (q.v.), have a divine kingship and elaborate political institutions. In the 19th century they were invaded and conquered by the Kololo (q.v.), a Sotho tribe, whose language they still speak. Eventually they managed to drive the invaders

out and established themselves as the dominant tribe in the area. National identity focuses on the person of the King and on the Princess Chief, his sister. Each of them maintains a separate court, one in the north, the other in the south of the country. The Lozi are famous for their complex legal and administrative machinery. They believe in a High God, the divine kingship and ancestral spirits.
(pages 26-29)

LUCHAZI *Population:* 60,000. Language: Bantu. The Luchazi live on the Angola-Zambia frontier and spread to the east as far as the Luena and Lunguebungu rivers. Most of their country is densely wooded. They keep only a few cattle but guinea pigs are bred for food as well as pigs introduced by the Europeans. They have markets at which they sell their surpluses of groundnuts, pigs' fat, dried fish and beeswax. They are primarily agriculturalists who grow millet and maize in rotation. Their settlements are small groups of mud and thatch huts arranged in a circle and stockaded. Four or five settlements will sometimes combine to form one large village of 200 or more huts under a single headman. Descent is traced through the maternal line and most homes consist of a mother and her children living under the protection of the woman's brother. Where the husband lives with his wife his first responsibility will nonetheless be towards his own sister's children. Children inherit the status and property of their maternal uncles although there are indications that fathers are increasingly asserting their rights over their wives and children under European influence. Divorce is easy in this society and women frequently practise abortion and contra-ception. Funerals are elaborate and ancestors are venerated.

LUENA *Population:* 90,000. Language: Bantu. Most Luena live in the area between the Luena and Kasai rivers. Well-watered plains cover much of their territory but a few villages are built on little islands in the middle of swamps. Fishing is more important than agriculture. Villages are often near lakes and rivers and are densely packed. The Luena have rapidly adapted to cash trading and the market system. Much of what they grow is sold to neighboring tribes or to Europeans. Most important are groundnuts, pulza oil, kidney cotton and rice. Their own staples are fish and cassava. Although dispersed over a

wide area they are a fairly homogeneous group ruled over by only one chief. Descent is traced through the mother's line and maternal uncles traditionally possess greater authority over young people than fathers. Marriages tend to be less stable than in other Bantu societies where substantial bride-prices are paid. Divorce is simple and women are said to practise contraception and abortion on a wide scale. Herbal medicine and exorcism are used to cure diseases. They believe in a High God who is associated with the weather and in the power of ancestral spirits.

LUIMBE *Population:* 40,000. Language: Bantu. The Luimbe live in the upper reaches of the River Kwanza, north of Vila General Machado, Angola. They live on a well-watered plain. They practise agriculture and keep chickens and cattle for slaughter. But mainly they derive their living from fishing. For centuries they have traced their ancestry through their mothers but lately there have been indications that they are changing to a patrilineal system in which authority is in the hands of a man's father rather than his mother's brother. They build their dwellings of mud and thatch. Small Luimbe villages are usually sited near sycamore trees. These trees are treated as memorials to dead chiefs and each tree is individually named and revered.

LUNDA The Lunda had a great Bantu empire in the 17th century and are now a group of related but independent tribes of central and southern Africa. The southern Lunda are represented here by Chokwe (q.v.), Luchazi (q.v.), Luena (q.v.), Mbunda (q.v.), Ndembu (q.v.).

MAHAFALY *Population:* 80,000. Language: Malagasy (Malayo-Polynesian). The Mahafaly are located in south-west Madagascar, bounded by Menarandra to the east and Ohilahy to the north. They share the southern coast of the island with the Antandroy (q.v.) with whom they have been continually at war. Their life style is very similar to that of the Sakalava (q.v.). They are pastoralists who live in isolated villages. Their huts are rectangular structures of straw with thatched gable roofs. They were once divided into four kingdoms and still retain a royal ancestor cult. Their religion centers on royal relics and on tombs that are decorated with

137

elaborate wood carvings. At one time they practised human sacrifice. A characteristic mortuary rite consisted of leaving the corpses of important personages to decompose in the open before burial.

MALAYS There are still pure-blooded Malays in South Africa, descended from Batavian rebels brought from the East Indies and enslaved by the Dutch in the 18th century. They are classified as Coloreds for political purposes, but in fact tend to be pure Malay, for by the end of the 18th century, when they arrived in South Africa, miscegenation by whites was rare: there were enough white women, and the practice became socially discredited. Before all slaves were released in 1837 the Malays were often house servants and coachmen. Now they are tradesmen, artisans, and businessmen.

MANALA *Population:* 30-40,000. Language: Bantu. The Manala live in central Transvaal north of Pretoria, South Africa. They are cattle herders who also grow maize. Their staple foods are maize porridge and milk products. They use their cows as 'capital' and rarely slaughter them. A strict cattle taboo is imposed on women. Men herd and milk the cattle while women tend the fields. Very stringent marriage regulations are imposed on the young. No one is allowed to marry within the clan. Villages are dispersed homesteads or *kraals*. A polygynous family often occupy a group of huts. Each of a man's wives is given her own hut where she cooks for her children. If a man dies without children it becomes the duty of his younger brother or other near kinsman to impregnate the dead man's widow. The children she bears are then ascribed to her deceased husband. Girls are valued as a means of increasing the family herd. The more daughters a man has the more cows she receives in bride-price when they marry. Manala religion centers on the placating of ancestral spirits. These spirits are thought to punish discord within the community and especially failure to discharge one's bridewealth obligations.

MANYIKA *Population:* 100,000. Language: Bantu. The Manyika live on both sides of the Rhodesia-Mozambique border between Umtali and Vila Manica. They form a part of the culturally homogeneous Shona nation (q.v.).

MASIKORD see SAKALAVA

MAURITIANS *Population:* 850,000. Languages: creole (an Africanized French patois), Hindi and other Indo-Pakistan languages, English. Mauritius, 720 square miles, lies in the Indian Ocean, 500 miles east of Madagascar. Uninhabited until the 18th century, it has since been a multi-ethnic society, as is evident from the variety of faces, languages and architectural styles on the island. Most of its inhabitants are Indians, but there are also Europeans, mainly of French and British descent, and creoles, Chinese, Malagasy, Negroes, Sinhalese, and Malays. The Portuguese discovered the island in the 16th century. In 1598 it was seized by the Dutch, who named it after Prince Maurice of Nassau. They abandoned it in 1710 but a few years later the French established a sugar-growing colony there and from this time onwards it began to prosper. It was acquired by the British in 1810 under the Treaty of Paris but the existing French laws and customs were retained so that the island remained French in character. Nearly half a million Indians were introduced as indentured labor between 1835 and 1907. Many of the Indians now work on the sugar plantations. Sugar is by far the most important export but now pineapples, tobacco, tea and rum are exported as well. **(pages 94-103)**

MERINA *Population:* 1,250,000. Language: Malagasy (Malayo-Polynesian). The Merina inhabit the central plateau of Madagascar around Tananarive. For a long time they have been the dominant group in the island. Originally wet-rice cultivators, they managed, towards the end of the 18th century to establish a kingdom that conquered nearly the whole of Madagascar. Today many Merina are traders, teachers and administrators. Racially they are a mixed group. The Malayo-Polynesian element – light brown skin and slightly mongoloid features – is strongest among the descendants of free men, while the negroid element is most marked in those descended from slaves. They build two-storey houses and order their lives within the house according to astrological points. The north-east is considered the most sacred direction and is associated with their ancestors. All of the Merina are now Christians, mainly Protestants, but the ancient tomb cult persists in many places. **(pages 86-93)**

MIKEA see SAKALAVA

NAMA see HOTTENTOT

NARON see BUSHMEN

NDAU *Population:* 75,000. Language: Bantu. The Ndau inhabit parts of Melsetter, Charter, Gutu and Bikita districts in Rhodesia and about a third of them live in Mozambique. Most are concentrated between Umtali and Chimanimani. Villages are often clustered around rivers and fishing plays a very important part in their economy. Culturally they form a part of the Shona nation (q.v.).

NDEBELE *Population:* 300,000. Language: Bantu. The Ndebele live in fertile undulating country around Bulawayo in Rhodesia. By conquest the Rhodesian Ndebele established a state in 1838 with complex political institutions, but their power ended with the defeat of the last great Ndebele chief,

Lobengula, in 1893. Today they look to local chiefs for leadership and live in dispersed hamlets where they keep cows and grow maize. Increasing numbers are leaving the land in order to find work in towns. Those who remain on their farms are going over to cash crops. The traditional Ndebele *kraal* or homestead consists of a circle of beehive-shaped huts grouped around an enclosure in which the cattle are kept. Descent is traced through the father but children are only counted as legitimate once a substantial bride-price in cows has been handed over to the wife's family. Until such payment has been made the offspring belong to their mother's family. Town-dwelling Ndebele usually insist on bride-price payments in cash. Although many tribesmen are Christian, traditional beliefs survive: they venerate ancestors, fear witchcraft and divine the causes of misfortune and disease.

NDEMBU *Population:* 37,000. Language: Bantu. Most Ndembu live on fertile plateaux 3-5,000 feet above sea level. Their tribal lands lie between Malonga and Didolo on the Katanga border and extend to the east as far as Kanzenze and Sakabindi in Central Angola. In the 19th century they were part of the Lunda Empire of Mwata Naweji and are still known as the Southern Lunda. They cultivate finger millet and cassava, but cattle are not important in their economy. Villages are usually small and are sited several miles apart. They trace descent through the maternal line and young men are free to live in any settlement where they are related to one of the elders. Usually, however, a young man will begin his adult life by farming his mother's brother's land. Every individual belongs to one of twelve named Lunda clans and has special obligations to render assistance and hospitality to any other member of his clan. Women retain membership of their natal clans even after marriage. Very small bridewealth payments are made at marriage and divorce is easy, but there are elaborate ceremonies at initiation and death. Religion centers on belief in a supreme being associated with the weather and on worship of the ancestors.

NEIKUM see BUSHMEN

NGUNI The Nguni are a great Bantu nation numbering several million people. They

represent the southernmost extension of the Bantu. Owing to their superior technology and political organization they have successfully displaced most of the aboriginal Khoisan-speaking people of South Africa. Today they occupy much of Natal and the Cape of Good Hope. They are divided into a number of independent tribes the most important of which are the Pondo (q.v.), Swazi (q.v.), Tembu (q.v.), Xhosa (q.v.), and Zulu (q.v.).
(pages 52-59, 14-25)

NGWATO *Population:* 50,000. Language: Bantu. The Ngwato inhabit extensive areas of northern Transvaal as far as the border of Rhodesia. They are agriculturalists for whom cattle is of great importance in marriage. In many respects they resemble the Sotho (q.v.).

NYANEKA-NKHUMBI *Population:* 80,000. Language: Bantu. The Nyaneka-Nkhumbi inhabit the high plateaux and hill country of

south-west Angola in the region known as Serra da Chela. Although their land is well-watered for most of the year they have suffered several severe droughts in recent years. They herd cattle and cultivate maize and sorghum from their widely dispersed family homesteads. A cluster of huts is built in horseshoe formation with the most prominent dwelling reserved for worshipping ancestors. They trace descent through the mother's line and a young man looks to his maternal uncle for his first cows and farming land. Every respected adult male possesses, in addition to his usual herd, two specially consecrated 'sacred cows'. One of these has been given to him by his father, the other by his mother's brother. These animals are dedicated respectively to his deceased paternal and maternal relatives. Special care is bestowed on them and their behavior is observed, for it is believed that the ancestors use them to communicate with the living. Girls keep round stones in their mouths from the time they reach puberty. These stones are called 'children' and are never taken out, not even while eating or sleeping. They are removed at marriage when it is hoped that they will be replaced by children. At puberty boys are circumcised and girls have elaborate geometric patterns tattooed on their abdomens. Religion centers on the worship of the ancestors.

OVIMBUNDU *Population:* 1,300,000. Language: Ovimbundu. The Ovimbundu live in the Benguella highlands of west-central Angola. The size of their settlements ranges from 5 to 500 households. Large villages are normally associated with royal residences. The Ovimbundu keep cattle mainly for prestige reasons, and large herds are owned only by chiefs. They derive most of their livelihood from agriculture and from hunting. Their staple crop is maize. Professional hunters are specially initiated but there are communal hunts during the dry season (June to July) when the entire village is involved. At that time of the year large tracts of land are covered in grass ten or more feet high. The people form a ring around about two square miles of grassland and set fire to it. Animals are killed with bows and arrows, spears and clubs as they rush from the flames. Game obtained in this way for food include antelope, snakes, foxes, wolves, mice, rabbits and leopards.

Blacksmiths are important in this society. Like hunters and diviners they pass their skills from father to son and entry into the profession is attended by special rituals. The 139

Ovimbundu were formerly grouped into 22 chiefdoms. About half of these were subject to more powerful rulers and a few of the chiefs were treated almost as sacred kings. There was a tradition of making war for plunder and tribute. Human sacrifice was known but not widely practised. Slavery survived until quite recently. Polygyny is practised, though now on a small scale. Commoners rarely have more than two wives while recent kings have had as many as twelve. Each wife has her own hut, granary and chickens. Children trace their descent through both the father's and the mother's line. Movable property is passed down from the mother's brother to the sister's son, while land and marriage cattle are obtained from one's father. They are ancestor worshippers. Spirit huts contain the skulls of former chiefs. There is a universal fear of the spirits of stillborn babies and mental defectives. Great precautions are taken to ward off the activities of sorcerers.

PEDI *Population:* 770,000. Language: Bantu. The Pedi are also known as the Transvaal Basotho. They live in Transvaal around Pretoria. Many today are employed as wage-laborers in European-run enterprises. Those who preserve their traditional way of life cultivate and herd cattle. They share many of the cultural traits of the Sotho (q.v.).

PONDO *Population:* 300,000. Language: Bantu. The Pondo inhabit the coastal area of South Africa just south of Zulu tribal lands. Agriculture and animal husbandry are equally important. Once part of the warlike Nguni tribes (q.v.) they are now sedentary people whose chiefs retain little of their former power. They live in dispersed family homesteads or *kraals:* cylindrical cone dwellings grouped round a space where cattle are kept. At marriage substantial payments of cattle are made to the bride's family. Where a wife fails to bear children or dies before her husband, it is customary for her family to provide the husband with another wife, preferably a sister of the one he paid bridewealth for. Descent is traced through the male line and all the inhabitants of a settlement are related to the senior kinsman who acts as spiritual and political leader of the community. There is a cattle taboo that forbids women any contact with cows. Religion centers on the spirits of the ancestors.

PORTUGUESE *Population:* 650,000. Language: Portuguese. Most Portuguese in southern Africa are relatively recent settlers of Portugal's two vast colonies, Mozambique and Angola, or are involved in the administration. They constitute about 5 per cent of the population. Although Portuguese sailors were the first to discover southern Africa and to establish communities (in the 15th century) they remained mainly on the coast until a century ago. There is a small minority of Portuguese in South Africa.

RONGA *Population:* 100,000. Language: Bantu. The Ronga inhabit an area of southern Mozambique around Lourenço Marques and extend southwards to the border of Natal Province, South Africa. They subsist primarily by cultivating sorghum and maize. They keep goats and chickens in all villages as well as cows. At one time they formed part of the culturally-homogeneous Thonga (q.v.) nation and recognized a paramount chief. This ruler was hedged by taboos and was killed if he developed the slightest physical defect, even the loss of a tooth. The authority of paramount chiefs has vanished under the influence of European control and most tribesmen are under the effective leadership only of local village headmen. Many Ronga have migrated to towns but those who preserve their traditional way of life live in dispersed hamlets of thatched huts grouped around cattle enclosures. Although they trace descent through the paternal line the influence of maternal relatives is strong. Children, especially, depend on their mothers' brothers at initiation and, later, at marriage. At one time the authority of the maternal uncle was so great that he could sell his nephews and nieces into slavery. There is a taboo that prevents women from coming in contact with cattle. Ronga religion centers on fire symbolism and ancestor worship.

ST MARIENS *Population:* 11,000. Language: Malagasy (Malayo-Polynesian stock). The St Mariens live on the island of Sainte Marie off the east coast of Madagascar. Their way of life resembles that of the Betsimisaraka but they represent a particularly mixed population that has come in turn under the influence of Polynesians, Arabs, European pirates and sailors of various nationalities, Africans and Indians. Today they are all Christians.

SAKALAVA *Population:* 355,000. Language: Malagasy (Malayo-Polynesian). The Sakalava occupy the whole western coast of Madagascar and are divided into four named groups: the Sakalava proper who are pastoralists, the Masikoro who are agriculturalists, the Vezo who are fishermen and a group of hunters and gatherers called Mikea. At one time the whole area was divided into several Sakalava kingdoms in each of which the ruling Sakalava dominated the other three groups. They lived in small, scattered settlements and the system of government operated through each region providing wives for their king. They have elaborate carved tombs which are noted, in some areas, for their erotic motifs. Religion centers around a royal cult and spirit possession ceremonies. Other beliefs are linked to personal healing ceremonies. Until the end of the 19th century they practised human sacrifice and the spirits of deceased kings were believed to possess the living.

SHONA *Population:* 1.5 million. Language group: Shona. Today Shona tribes occupy most of Rhodesia and Mozambique where they cultivate the high veldt and the low veldt valleys. Those who live in the northern

districts of Rhodesia, like the Korekore, live in low grasslands infested by tsetse flies, while those who have settled along the border of Rhodesia and Mozambique, notably the Manyika, have built their settlements along perennial streams and in forests. In the pre-colonial era all Shona were united under a paramount chief who was treated as a divine king. The complexity of their government and their ability to expand rapidly at the expense of smaller, less powerful groups made them famous.

Today nothing remains of the Shona kingdom. Tribesmen are under the authority of local headmen or minor chiefs. Most villages are no more than dispersed hamlets. Round huts of wattle and daub are grouped around a central plaza in which a sacred tree grows. The Shona recognize two forms of marriage: one involves the payment of substantial bride-price in cattle, the other mode involves only a token gift of a few hoes and a lengthy period of pre-marital and post marital bride service by the husband. Everywhere agriculture is more important than animal husbandry. They subsist primarily by growing sorghum or maize with millet, eleusine, rice, beans and peanuts as subsidiary crops. Descent is traced through the paternal line although a few Shona groups may be matrilineal, tracing their descent and inheriting property through the mother. Initiation schools, common to so many other Bantu tribes, do not exist among the Shona and in most groups males are not circumsised. They have totemic clans which hold certain animals in special reverence, and will not eat them. Those whose totem is the crocodile believe that the rivers would dry up if one crocodile were shot. Women and children are forbidden contact with corpses and women are not allowed to approach cattle. The Shona are well known as musicians and makers of drums and wind instruments. They have an elaborate cult to the Supreme Being whom they regard as the creator of mankind. This being manifests himself in great natural phenomena like volcanic eruptions. There are also tribal gods and ancestral spirits.

SIHANAKA *Population:* 125,000. Language: Malagasy (Malayo-Polynesian). The Sihanaka live around Lake Alaotra in north-central Madagascar. They have mixed a great deal with their neighbors the Merina (q.v.) and the Betsimisaraka (q.v.). Isolated groups of Sihanaka are fishermen, others cultivate rice and some practise animal husbandry. The fishermen use dugout canoes. They are less rigidly stratified into classes than their neighbors. Circumcision is performed on all boys and is attended by elaborate rituals which include a contest between young men and bulls and the eating of the severed foreskin by the maternal uncle. They were also known for long drawn-out funeral ceremonies. Until fairly recently polygamy was practised on a wide scale but this is now dying out. Tomb cults survive.

SOTHO *Population:* 1,400,000. Language: Bantu. The Sotho are mountain people living in the high grasslands of Lesotho and adjoining areas of South Africa. Cultivators of maize, they have almost universally replaced the hoe with ox-drawn plows. Cattle herding and sheep farming are most important to their economy. The grazing requirements of herds and flocks make it necessary to move from the grasslands of the high plateaux in the summer to the low veldt in the winter. They also do a considerable amount of collecting and gathering. Edible earths, clays, medicinal herbs and plants of all kinds supplement the staple diet of maize and dairy food. They live in tiny settlements of rarely more than 50 people. It is said that the largest village of Basutoland contains but 700 souls. At one time they were the core group of a Sotho nation which incorporated more than a dozen big tribes including the Lovedu (q.v.), the Pedi (q.v.) and the Venda (q.v.). Remnants of their conquest state are still detected in the manner in which they classify tribesmen – according to sex, age grade, rank (i.e. commoner or aristocrat). Clear distinction is also made between 'pure' Sotho and those descended from incorporated tribes. They have a paramount chief to whom all Sotho owe allegiance. He gives individuals the right to build homesteads and administers tribal law. They trace descent through the paternal line. Most marriages are monogamous although polygamy remains the ideal. If a man's wife is barren she can take a maidservant with whom the husband has intercourse. Children resulting from such a union are legitimate and inherit the family property. Christianity was introduced early in the 19th century but has not resulted in widespread conversion. Beliefs in magic and divination abound. They attribute sickness to sin or witchcraft and healers have an important position in society. Most of the cult activity centers on ancestral spirits. Sotho women tattoo their faces.

SWAZI *Population:* 300,000. Language: Bantu. The Swazi inhabit the high *veldt* and the coastal lowlands of Swaziland and the immediately adjoining areas of Transvaal and Mozambique. The entire area of the country measures only 120 miles with a maximum breadth of 90 miles. In the north of Swaziland there are mountains that rise to an altitude of 6,000 feet. Maize and sorghum are cultivated on high ridges or terraces. Agriculture and animal husbandry are

141

equally important in their economy.

Until the 19th century the Swazi were a warlike people headed by a fighting king and a strong tribal army. The society is still divided into commoners and aristocrats. The latter live in large homesteads which may contain up to 25 inhabitants including the headman, his mother, several wives and their children. Each wife will have her own cooking, sleeping and storage huts separated from the other dwellings of the homestead by a reed fence. Each woman also has her own plot where she grows crops for her family. Blacksmiths and specialists in ritual occupy privileged positions. The Swazi keep cattle for prestige, more than for food. The head of each family acts as the priest in the ancestor cult. The status of the living is carried over into the next life: the ancestors of kings are given great honor while those of commoners are treated with considerably less ceremony. They are accomplished musicians whose favorite instrument is six-stringed and evolved from a hunting bow. They also use different kinds of rattles and shields as percussion instruments. Christian missionaries have been active since the beginning of the century and one result of their presence has been the emergence of several separatist churches led by African 'prophets' who combine Christian and traditional elements in their cults. The royal ancestor cult and the personification of the elements survive to this day. Even Christian Swazi are said to believe that the king has the power to produce rain.
(pages 52-59)

TANALA *Population:* 225,000. Language: Malagasy (Malayo-Polynesian). The Tanala inhabit the highland forests that overlook the east coast of Madagascar. Most of them live at 3,000-4,000 feet above sea level in forests that are well watered but poor in game. The area is rich in iron and the Tanala supplement slash-and-burn cultivation with exploitation of the natural resources of their forests. Their principal crop is coffee but they also cultivate rice. They are skilled blacksmiths who forge their own tools and weapons. Although the environment is not suited to livestock they keep some cattle for prestige reasons. The meat is hardly ever eaten and even the milk is only taken if there is more than the calves can use. They do not even use the manure for fertilizer. The Tanala live in small self-contained groups. They see themselves as opposed to the plateau people whom they consider inferior. They bury their

dead in hollowed-out rocks. They accept homosexuality and transvestism. They believe in a supreme god or spirit and numerous non-human spirits who dwell in streams and forests. Most of their worship is directed to ancestral ghosts and there is a certain amount of spirit and ghost possession.
(pages 68-71)

TAWARA *Population:* several thousand. Language: Bantu. The Tawara inhabit parts of Darwin district and the eastern portions of the Chinimanda Reserve in Rhodesia. They share the culture and traditions of the Shona people (q.v.). They are extremely poor. Unable to keep cattle because their land is infested by the tsetse fly, they live by cultivating sorghum and by fishing in rivers and swamps. Most of them are patrilineal but in the extreme north of their territory some groups trace descent through the maternal line. Pierced lips and lip clips are characteristic of the tribe.

TEMBU *Population:* 20,000. Language: Bantu. The Tembu live in the Umtata district of Cape Province, South Africa. They were once part of the Nguni (q.v.) nation but are now led by local headmen. A great many of them work in the gold mines of South Africa. Those who remain on their tribal territory keep cattle but subsist mainly from agriculture. Cows are used for bridewealth payments although this is now being replaced by payments in cash to the bride's family. Women cultivate the fields where they grow maize. Since the first European contact they have kept goats, sheep and dogs as well as horses, donkeys and pigs. The women wear aprons and necklaces made of beads. Marriage rules are strictly enforced and there are several categories of kin that one may not marry. Widows are inherited by their dead husbands' younger brothers. Religion consists of ancestor worship.
(pages 52-59)

THONGA The Thonga are a great Bantu nation of southern Africa numbering well over one million people. They live to the south of the Shona people and occupy parts of Mozambique. They are represented by the Bathonga (q.v.), the Chopi (q.v.) and the Ronga (q.v.).

TONGA *Population:* 200,000. Language: Bantu. There are three principal groups of Tonga: the Plateau Tonga or Northern Tonga who inhabit the Mazabuka district north of Choma extending as far as the Kafue river in Zambia; the Southern Tonga, or Toka, who extend as far south as Sesheke on the Zambia-Botswana border; and the Valley Tonga, or We, of the lower Zambezi valley. They cultivate maize and sorghum as staples and beans and ground nuts as subsidiary crops. Many of them are now cash croppers, using the slash-and-burn system. Villages tend to be small. Settlements are founded by men who are related through the maternal line and it is usual for all the males in a village to claim descent from a single matrilineal ancestor. The kin group is tied by exceptionally strong bonds. Collective responsibility obliges kinsmen to pay one another's debts. The people are grouped into clans each of which is associated with some animal or plant. Yet no one avoids or honors the totem in any way. The main function of the clan system is to regulate marriages. It is forbidden to marry within one's own clan. Funerals are occasions for large gatherings of relatives. At such times cows are slaughtered, guns are fired over the grave and there is much dancing and beating of drums. The spirits of the dead are believed to enter the living. There are rain shrines and rain ceremonies. No disharmony is tolerated during these rites. It is believed droughts are the result of unresolved conflict in the community. Many sorts of charms are used to counter the dangers of witchcraft.

TSIMIHETY *Population:* about 392,000. Language: Malagasy (Malayo-Polynesian). The Tsimihety occupy the interior of the northern part of the island of Madagascar. They live in compact villages and build rectangular huts with walls of reeds or mats and gabled, thatched roofs. They are agriculturalists and pastoralists. The society is divided into named clans and subdivided into castes. In family life the role of the mother's eldest brother is of particular importance. Otherwise, in culture and belief, they resemble many other Malagasy societies.

TSWANA *Population:* 800,000. Language: Bantu. The Tswana live on the grassy fringes of the Kalahari desert in the modern state of Botswana. The Tswana people are divided into eight tribes, each under its own chief. They herd cattle and cultivate maize and millet. Formerly they were organized into a powerful conquering state geared to the assimilation of conquered tribes and refugee groups. Today the personal names of people still indicate whether they are of pure Tswana origin or descendants of attached groups. Unlike the Pedi or the Venda to whom they are related, the Tswana often live in large towns with populations of 5,000 or more. Men are divided into age sets which formed the basis for military regiments. Chiefs would enlist these regiments not only for fighting but also to perform public services. In recent times age sets have been ordered to round up stray cattle and to go into wage labor in South African mines. Money earned by these men would be handed over to their chief. The power of the chief rests largely on his willingness to redistribute his wealth in public feasts and ceremonies. The religion of the Tswana centers on the worship of ancestral spirits.

VENDA *Population:* about 135,000. Language: Bantu. The Venda live in the Transvaal near the border with Rhodesia. Agriculture is more important to them than animal husbandry. They keep cows but do not observe the usual ritual separation of women and cattle. Their culture is in very many respects similar to that of the Shona (q.v.).

VEZO see SAKALAVA (and pages 76-85)

XHOSA (XOSA) *Population:* 2 million. Language: Bantu. The Xhosa are concentrated in the area of East London in the Cape Province of South Africa. They were famous as a warlike people who waged a long war against the Boers. Today they live in dispersed homesteads or *kraals* where they keep cattle and cultivate maize as well as some beans, millet, sweet potatoes and watermelons. The women are distinguished by the red ocher they paint on their faces and stain their blankets and undergarments with. Both sexes wear earrings and are heavy pipe smokers. The top joint of the little finger is severed from the left hand. The cattle complex is very highly developed among them. Women are forbidden any contact with cows. It is the men who milk the cows, a task they perform naked. Nor are women allowed to touch milk. At meal times it is the men who distribute milk to the family. In burial ceremonies there is a rigid separation of the sexes. Men are buried in or near cattle byres or in a graveyard reserved for male corpses. Women are not allowed to look upon a male corpse. Men and women share the same hut subject only to the rule that men sleep on the right and women on the left side of the hut. Husbands and wives wishing to have intercourse are required to leave the dwelling. Wealthy men may take several wives but

only one of these is given full marital status. They worship their tribal ancestors and sacrifice oxen to them.
(pages 52-59)

ZEZURU *Population:* 150,000. Language: Bantu. The Zezuru live in the undulating highland districts of Mazoe, Lomagundi, Salisbury, Hartley, Marandelas and Charter in Rhodesia. They are culturally and historically a part of the Shona nation (q.v.), although many are wage laborers who make up much of the slum population of Rhodesian towns.

ZULU *Population:* about 2 million. Language: Bantu. The Zulu live in Natal in an area bounded by the Pongola river and the St Lucia estuary to the north, the Tugela river to the south, the Indian Ocean to the east and the Drakensberg mountains to the west. They grow maize and keep large herds of cattle. During the 19th century they became a powerful nation who successfully plundered surrounding tribes, especially the Swazi. The warrior king, Shaka, gained absolute power by instituting a full-time army of unmarried men. The military strength of the Zulu ended with the defeat they suffered at the hands of the British in 1880. Since then and in spite of almost a century of white domination, the Zulu have retained their tribal identity and loyalty to their chief. They are divided into numerous clans. Their villages are usually small and associated with a group of men who trace their descent from a single named ancestor. Cattle are used for bride-price. Once the wife's family has taken possession of the cows the wife's fertility is ascribed to the husband's family. And all children born to her, even if they were conceived in adultery or after her husband's death, are ascribed to him. The Zulu are polygamous and marriage with two sisters is especially approved. If a wife dies childless she is replaced by a younger sister. If this is not possible, some of the marriage cattle are returned to her husband's family. Various religious and magical rites are performed by the king and by rainmakers. There is also an elaborate ancestor cult.
(pages 14-25)

All population figures are approximate.